D0651586

MIND POWER

MIND POWER

GETTING WHAT YOU
WANT THROUGH
MENTAL TRAINING

Bernie Zilbergeld, Ph.D.
Arnold A. Lazarus, Ph.D.

LITTLE, BROWN AND COMPANY   Boston   Toronto

FIRST EDITION

For reasons of privacy, many of the names
in this book have been changed.

Library of Congress Cataloging-in-Publication Data
Zilbergeld, Bernie.
    Mind Power.

    Bibliography: p.
    1. Success.   2. Mental discipline.   3. Imagery
(Psychology)   I. Lazarus, Arnold A.   II. Title.
BF637.S8Z55   1987   158'.1   87-4149
ISBN 0-316-98790-5

RRD OH

*Published simultaneously in Canada
by Little, Brown & Company (Canada) Limited*

PRINTED IN THE UNITED STATES OF AMERICA

To the memory of our parents,
Clara and Sam Zilbergeld,
Rachael and Benjamin Lazarus

CONTENTS

ACKNOWLEDGMENTS

We are grateful for the support and comments of a number of colleagues and friends, including Lonnie Barbach, Carol Ellison, Jackie Hackel (who claims she never would have gotten her middle-aged body up Mount Kilimanjaro without the mental training she did after reading an early draft of this book), Cory Hammond, Howard LaGardé, Carolyn Saarni, Ann Schifter, Sandy Vogl, and Robyn Young. Special thanks are due to Gerald Edelstien and Dianne Morrisette, who went through all of the many drafts and always gave wonderful advice, some of which we even followed. We are indebted to Daphne Ann Lazarus for suggesting the title and to two excellent advisers, editor Bill Phillips and copy editor Michael Brandon.

ACKNOWLEDGMENTS

MIND POWER

It is the mind that maketh good or ill,
That maketh wretch or happy, rich or poor.
                              — Edmund Spenser

CHAPTER 1

THE POWERS OF THE MIND

We all have minds but most of us don't do much with them. We put in a lot of information about external tasks — driving, typing, selling, taking inventory — and not much else. Most of us assume there's not much that can be done about the mind. If it shows us lots of depressing pictures, we go around feeling depressed. If it keeps telling us about inadequacies and faults, we go around feeling powerless and bad. If it keeps repeating that we can't do this and won't do that, we assume that's just how it is.

It doesn't occur to us that we can change the images and thoughts. It seems natural to accept what our minds provide. "That's just the way I am," we say. We don't understand that it has nothing to do with what's natural. It has to do only with who's in charge.

Minds do what they are programmed to do, though much of the programming is unintended. If you were belittled as a child, chances are good that your mind will have recorded all those humiliations and will play them back at every opportunity. If your parents' relationship was cold and distant, chances are that your mind will arrange internal images and phrases guiding you in that same direction. If you once had a bad experience with arithmetic, your mind may have decided to keep you away from anything having to do with numbers by evoking anxiety whenever you approach the subject. So here you are, ten, twenty, thirty or more years later, still telling yourself that you can't do math and making it impossible to give it a chance. Much of the mind's "natural" programming consists of such self-imposed limitations that keep you from realizing your potential and from feeling good about yourself.

But you don't have to be stuck with how your mind has been programmed. If your Bergman-like mental movies are too depressing, you can have the Marx Brothers, *Ghostbusters, Chariots of Fire,* or something else. If you're tired of hearing what a dolt you are or all the things you should fear, you can have your mind play back the most loving and supportive internal tapes you want, and with the kind of music you intentionally choose. You've heard enough of limitations and inabilities; you can now hear of strengths and possibilities. You've seen enough gloomy prospects; you can now have brightly lit vistas. You can now take control of your mind instead of letting it control you. You can become your own programmer and manage your mind's productions, running movies and playing tapes that please and empower you.

A great deal of what we have learned about the powers of the mind comes from an unexpected source — champion athletes. The 1984 Olympics demonstrated over and over the effectiveness of mental training. We saw bobsled teams sway as they practiced visualizing before each event. We heard gymnast Mary Lou Retton tell how she "mind-scripted" every move the night before winning her gold medal. We read how Greg Louganis, another gold medalist and the only diver ever to score a perfect 10 in international competition, employed as much mental preparation as physical training. He visualized each dive as he wanted it to be, step by step, forty times before mounting the platform. Similar stories about the value of mental training were told by skiers, weight lifters, hurdlers, boxers, and just about everyone else.

It isn't only Olympic champions who have been using their heads. It seems that almost every great athlete and coach has been saying something good about using the mind. Basketball star Bill Russell and golfer Jack Nicklaus wrote persuasively of the importance of mental training to their play. Psychologist Charles Garfield wrote that the great athletes he studied "acknowledge that 60 to 90 percent of success in sports is due to mental factors." Dallas Cowboy coach Tom Landry noted, "However you think determines how you play," and Billie Jean King warned, "If you believe you will fail, you will find some way to fail." And from a sport where some people expect to hear nothing at all about the mind, bodybuilding, came the voice of Arnold Schwarzenegger, the greatest bodybuilder of all time. He called the mind a dynamo, a source of vital energy. "That energy can be negative and work against you," he wrote, "or you can harness it to give yourself unbelievable workouts and build a physique that lives up to your wildest expectations." The athlete advocates of mental training have included such past and present standouts as Fran Tarkenton, Bruce Jenner, Marilyn King, John Brody, Jim Brown, O. J. Simpson, Chris Evert Lloyd, Martina Navratilova, Jean-Claude Killy, Pelé, Bill Walton, Steve Carlton, and Mary Decker.

There have been more than just testimonials. Studies done in the United States, the Soviet Union, and elsewhere support what the players and coaches have been saying. Training the mind is at least as important as training the body.

If mental training were useful only to athletes, it would be an interesting fact of limited importance. But evidence is pouring in from all areas of life. Consider these examples:

• Psychologist and avid skier Lonnie Barbach pulled the ligaments in her left knee while skiing and spent a painful six weeks on crutches. Two years later, she injured her right knee in the same way and to the same extent. This time she used the mental training she had learned since her first injury. For two weeks she imagined her ligaments tightening and a decrease in swelling, soreness, and pain. There were no crutches this time and she was healed in less than three weeks.

• As if to prove that Barbach wasn't hallucinating, researchers Larry Moore and Gerald Kaplan used mental training to give suggestions for increased blood flow to one side of the body to patients with equal burn damage on both sides of their bodies. The results clearly demonstrated that increased blood flow to the target side was achieved and, more important, that healing was quicker on that side. This study, one of many with similar results, clearly supports what Barbach and many others have found for themselves: the mind can affect the body in important ways.

• As if to prove that none of the people mentioned above was hallucinating, we heard from our utterly practical and levelheaded editor at Little, Brown, Bill Phillips, who tore the ligaments in one shoulder in a bicycle accident. Recalling what we said about Lonnie Barbach's injury, he used some of the methods in this book to promote healing and deal with the pain. He called to tell us and exclaimed, in a more excited voice than we had heard in ten years of working with him: "This stuff really works!" This is not scientific evidence, of course, but coming from a man like Bill Phillips, it means something.

• Many years ago, a young William Paley became president of CBS when it had no stations of its own, was losing money, and was insignificant in the broadcasting business. What Paley had, as David Halberstam described it, was "a sense of vision, a sense of what might be." He could see millions of Americans in the hinterlands with almost no form of entertainment other than radio and was confident he could offer them something. "He could envision the audience at a time when there was in fact no audience." Within ten years, CBS had 114 radio stations and was earning almost $30 million. More than forty years later, with Paley again in charge, CBS is a dominant force in broadcasting.

• Before performing a new surgical procedure or one he hasn't had much experience with, nationally known urologist Ira Sharlip sits back in his chair, closes his eyes, and imagines going through every step. If he has trouble imagining any step, he realizes he will have trouble with it in the operating room, so he consults a reference book, an experienced colleague, or a teaching videotape until he can imagine it smoothly. He credits this technique with making him a better surgeon.

• In training for a different kind of performance, Olympic diving champion Greg Louganis uses mental training to improve his singing, dancing, and acting, as he prepares for a career in show business.

• Dr. Jill Caire of San Francisco's Pacific Medical Center uses mental training in many areas of her life. She used it to stop smoking and to overcome a blood phobia so strong that she once fainted upon noticing a drop of blood on the dressing of a hospitalized friend. The cure has been so effective that Dr. Caire now uses similar procedures to reduce patient distress during medical procedures such as lumbar puncture and bone marrow aspiration, during which she is present. She also uses mental training "to help me focus my attention and write enjoyably," quite a change for a woman who used to hate to write.

The evidence has been mounting that training the mind is of great benefit in almost every area of human endeavor. The research of people such as Charles Garfield has made it clear that superior achievers in all aspects of life, including business and finance, make heavy use of mental training. Corporate superstars such as Thomas Watson, the man who founded IBM, and John Sculley, president of Apple Computer, are but two examples. Garfield has found that peak performers use their minds differently than other people. These different ways can be learned. More and more businesses have been using mental-training courses for their executives and salespeople for the simple reason that these courses lead to improved performance.

The evidence has also been mounting that the mind plays a pivotal role in health and illness. Stress, often the result of how the mind perceives what needs to be done, how quickly, and to what degree of perfection, has been linked to all kinds of illnesses. Stress reduction can be achieved through retraining the mind, which leads to better habits and health. Depression, one of the most common disorders in America, has been shown in clinical studies to be largely a product of maladaptive thinking, and to be successfully treatable by mental training. Increasing evidence confirms that the mind is primary. As cognitive therapists have repeatedly demonstrated in the laboratory and the consulting office, in most cases our thoughts and mental images determine our feelings and behavior. Change the ideas and images, and feelings and action also change.

Many of the popular psychotherapies of the 1960s and 1970s, which focused on the awareness and expression of feeling, have been supplanted by more cognitively oriented treatments that focus on reprogramming the mind. Cognitive behavior therapy, primarily a way of changing what you say to yourself and how you view yourself, has become one of the leading therapies and has influenced practitioners of other therapeutic schools.

From the corporate boardroom to the athletic field to the psychotherapist's and physician's office, using the mind to improve performance and the quality of life is finally coming into its own. More and more people in different fields are recognizing that the mind can be used to reprogram itself, leading to greater creativity, productivity, and satisfaction. The methods of mental training can be used to resolve emotional and behavioral problems, to achieve personal growth, and to enhance performance. The same techniques can be used with equal success in all these areas. They really come down to helping people be more effective in all aspects of their lives.

Two dramatic events from the world of sports well illustrate the powers of the mind. The first occurred in 1954. Before May 6 of that year, no one had ever run a mile in under four minutes; lots of runners had tried and many had come close, but there was a barrier. Many runners and scholars argued that the barrier was physiological, that human bodies simply couldn't run that fast. As Roger Bannister, the first human to break the barrier, said, "Everyone used to think it was quite impossible, and beyond the reach of any runner." But Bannister never thought this himself and prepared accordingly. What is perhaps even more astonishing than Bannister's own achievement is that once he proved it could be done, others were also able to do it. By now hundreds of runners have run a mile in less than four minutes. It is doubtful that human physiology underwent a significant change in that period. What is far more likely is that before Bannister's accomplishment, the self-limiting notion that a four-minute mile was impossible made it impossible. Once Bannister proved it was possible, something changed in the minds of other runners.

A similar thing happened in weight lifting. Before Vasily Alexeev lifted 501 pounds in 1970, no one had ever lifted 500 pounds over his head and many argued that it was a physiological impossibility. But in the month after Alexeev broke the barrier, four other weight lifters lifted over 500 pounds. By now, scores have done it. Why? The analysis of Arnold Schwarzenegger is undoubtedly correct. "They believed it was possible. The body didn't change. How could the body change that much? It was the same body. But the mind was different. Mentally it's possible to break records. Once you understand that, you can do it."

But what does this have to do with you? Probably a great deal, because your mind is no different from those of runners and weight lifters. The mind's double-edged power is at work in all of us, either hindering and making us miserable or facilitating our efforts and making us feel good. Your mind keeps you from doing things it doesn't believe are possible, but once it accepts that you can do something, chances are good you will be able to do it (provided, of course, that you are also prepared in other ways). This idea has ramifications in all of life.

Take a man who tells himself he doesn't have what it takes to give a good talk, one of the most common fears in America, and imagines the audience laughing at his attempts. He is depressed and distraught and not surprisingly gives a poor presentation even though he knows his material. Another man who also knows his material tells himself the opposite. He thinks he can give a good talk, and imagines himself doing so and the audience responding positively; not surprisingly, he greatly improves the chances of giving a good presentation. The difference between the first man and the second is only in how they use their minds.

But, you may be thinking, some things are absolute. Pain, for example, is pain, and it makes no difference what your mind says about it. But that is not quite the case. The experience of pain is very much influenced by what your mind is doing. Take two women in a dentist's office, both of whom are having exactly the same procedure. One woman has been terrified for days in advance, anticipating unendurable pain. Assuming that she gets to and stays in the office, she focuses on everything the dentist does, waiting for the horrible feelings to begin. As soon as the dentist touches her mouth, she feels profound anxiety and pain. Needless to say, she has a horrible experience. Even novocaine may not help much.

But the other woman has a very different kind of experience. Because she knows how to use the powers of her mind (what this book will teach you), she doesn't anticipate difficulty. Going to the dentist for her is no different than going shopping or brushing her hair, just something that needs to be done. She uses what she knows about the mind to cope with the dentist's drilling. Her experience is largely one of comfort.

Consider two people of equal abilities, appearance, and interests. One learns to deal with the inherent problems of close relationships and develops one that is the envy of friends; the other doesn't. One becomes very wealthy; the other doesn't. One goes to the top of his or her field; the other doesn't. Luck may have something to do with it, of course, but the main difference between those who make it and those who don't has to do with the powers of the mind and how they are used. The terms commonly used to describe the differences between these two groups — words like drive, motivation, competitiveness, confidence, will, perseverance, and belief in self — are all qualities of mind. The difference between winning and losing in business, sports, or elsewhere has less to do with the state of your quadriceps or your natural abilities than with the state of your mind.

We say of great pianists, surgeons, and pass catchers that they have great hands. But lots of people have great hands and very few become great surgeons, pianists, or wide receivers. The difference between those who do and those who don't is not in the hands.

In almost every single area of life that we can think of, the mind is what makes the difference between success and failure or between getting by and doing great. This holds true even in such a personal area as sexuality. The quantity and quality of your sex life — how much desire, arousal, and satisfaction you experience, and how well you function — is far more dependent on what is between your ears than what is between your legs.

This book is about the human mind and how it can help us get what we want. The mind, especially the parts of it that imagine and talk to us, is what programs us for success or failure. The human mind is the most complex and most marvelous tool ever created, far more powerful than any computer or other machine devised by man, and it influences everything we do. It is always active, with or without our awareness of it, and it cuts both ways: either to facilitate accomplishment of our goals or to block it.

Since the mind is always working anyway, why not make it work to your advantage?

There is a method, really a group of related methods, readily available, easy to learn, and simple to use on your own, that harness natural abilities we all have and that are amazingly effective. These methods have not received the attention they deserve. They have been presented in ways that have appealed to some people but have repulsed many others. They have been ensconced in metaphysical, religious, or psychobabble mumbo jumbo, making them difficult to understand and also unacceptable to many people.

THE POWERS OF THE MIND

The purpose of this book is to give these methods their proper attention, to explain what they are and how to use them, and to make them available to readers to use for whatever healthful and constructive ends they desire.

These methods are called by various names: *mental practice, mental training, mental rehearsal, mindscripting, visualization, guided imagery,* and *self-hypnosis.* They are related to other methods with names such as *relaxation training, autogenic training,* and *meditation.* All of these methods aspire to better use the inherent powers of the human mind. In order to avoid confusion, we use the term *mental training* to refer to our methods except in chapter 3, where we deal with some of the myths about hypnosis that affect the perception of all mental training. Although not especially catchy, we like the term *mental training* because it says it all: our methods will help you train your mind to get what you want.

Although we would have preferred simply to present the methods along with suggestions on how to use them to best effect, we cannot overlook the fact that there is still some resistance to them. Many Americans are suspicious of using the imagination and of *hypnosis,* one of the terms that describes the methods we teach. Rather than ignore the issue, we intend to spend some time on the misconceptions about our methods. We hope this will clear the air not only for those with doubts, but also for some who like the idea of reprogramming the mind but aren't sure exactly what it means.

We will reduce the methods to their basics. We will show that mental training is nothing but a systematic and disciplined use of natural abilities. It does not require exotic paraphernalia, particular religious or philosophical beliefs, strange vocabulary, or belief in much of anything at all except in the power of your own mind.

Our book is technique- rather than problem-oriented.

We have separated the main techniques into a few categories and devote a chapter to each. This way you can see what methods are available and how you want to use them. We assume readers are intelligent enough to apply the information to themselves in ways that make sense and best fit their particular preferences and goals. The best program is simply one that works for you; sooner or later everyone using a program of any sort has to tailor it to his or her particular situation. One reason that so many programs fail — whether they are called education, coaching, psychotherapy, or self-help — is that they try to fit everyone into the same mold. Yet we know these molds don't work for lots of people. Arnold Schwarzenegger, for instance, found that many of the standard bodybuilding exercises didn't do much for him. He had to substitute other exercises. Organizing the book as we have makes it easy for you to pick what makes most sense for you.

Both of us are licensed psychologists who have used these techniques, as well as many others, for a combined total of almost fifty years. As some readers already know from our previous writings, we are also both skeptical and cautious. We do not easily accept claims of great effectiveness and remarkable results from any therapeutic technique. We always want to know what the evidence is. Perhaps it says something about the methods in question that both of us have been persuaded of their power and usefulness in our work with patients, in our own lives, and by the research done by others. We say without any hesitation that these methods do work, and in the final chapter we give examples of how we used them to deal with crises in our own lives.

But there are two qualifications. The first is that they work only when used properly and consistently. Reading this book will give you the information you need to apply the methods to your life, but reading alone will not make the changes you desire. The time needed for the proper application of these methods is not great, especially when compared to the time usually spent in psychotherapy and other activities designed to improve performance, but some time, some effort, and some energy are necessary. If you are unwilling to invest the time and energy, there is no point in reading further. You are interested in magic and that is not what we have to offer.

On the other hand, if you are willing to take some time and expend some energy, read on. What is in the following pages may not make you another Mary Lou Retton (unless you are already a very fine gymnast), another Luciano Pavaroti (unless you already have an exquisite voice), a brilliant scholar (unless you are already very good), or a millionaire (unless you already know some things about making money), but there's every reason to believe that the information and methods presented will allow you to get more of what you want from life.

In most of the people we know, whether as clients, colleagues, or friends, the main barriers to greater achievement and happiness are of their own making. We see perfectly acceptable, even handsome and beautiful people, telling themselves no one could ever want them. We see those with great abilities mired in self-defeating images and ideas. We see those who have accomplished much in the past telling themselves they can no longer do anything. What they tell themselves is what holds them back. With some changes in how they perceive themselves, they could indeed do what they want. Not everything perhaps, but some things. We do not preach perfection, merely enhancement and improvement.

The second qualification is that although our methods have been successfully used by men and women with severe emotional problems, we have written the book for basically normal people who want to extend their capabilities. Those suffering from psychosis, those who have been hospitalized in the last few years for psychological or behavioral problems, those with serious chemical dependencies, and those who are suicidal should not attempt to use what's in this book except under the guidance of a professional therapist.

Our book is structured in such a way that you will benefit most from reading it all the way through, including the exercises and scripts, *before* trying any of the techniques (except for goal setting and relaxing). In the next two chapters we discuss the myths and realities of mental training and try to say why some people have been reluctant to believe in it. Chapter 4 is about setting goals, a crucial step in using the training effectively, and chapter 5 gives the nuts-and-bolts information you'll need to use the methods. In the rest of the book, chapters 6 through 12, we provide the techniques, giving information and examples to allow you to adapt them for yourself. There are also four "interludes." The first and last of these contain examples of mental training that are of special interest: one on stress management and one on dealing with anger. The second and third interludes contain optional exercises. While you may be tempted to turn immediately to the chapters that describe the methods, we ask you to resist the urge and first read what comes before them. As we said, this book is designed so that you will pick up what you need to know by reading the chapters in order. The information in the early ones is helpful to applying the techniques in the later ones.

As you go through the book, remember that you already possess the most powerful tool in the world for personal change. Your mind awaits you.

Compared to what we ought to be, we are only half awake. We are making use of only a small part of our physical and mental resources. The human individual possesses power of various sorts which he habitually fails to use.

— William James

CHAPTER 2

WHAT MENTAL TRAINING IS

You may be surprised at how simple mental training is, provided you're willing to let go of mystical notions and misunderstandings you may have picked up in the media. It is easy to understand and easy to use.

In a nutshell, mental training is simply a way of re-programming the mind to achieve more positive behaviors, feelings, and results. Although Western culture, especially American culture, is action-oriented and suspicious of "just sitting," "just thinking," and "just daydreaming," we are quickly learning that the mind's activity is paramount. How the mind receives, perceives, and interprets information determines what you think, how you feel, and what you do. We are beginning to understand that the mind can contribute to physical illness such as high blood pressure, heart disease, ulcers, asthma, and colitis. We are also beginning to understand that with different programming, the mind can heal such maladies. In recent years, our most rigorous scientists, physicists, have come to the defense of the imagination. More and more we hear of the use of fantasy and imaging in scientific discovery. The scientist we most revere, Albert Einstein, never conducted an experiment and was rarely inside a laboratory; he just sat and used his mind. He said that his imagination — he pictured himself riding on a beam of light — provided the key to his discovery of the theory of relativity. No wonder Einstein maintained that "imagination is more important than knowledge."

The essence of mental training is a state called *trance,* a natural human capacity consisting primarily of a state of focused attention in which we are more receptive than usual to suggestion. This state often comes about spontaneously, where it is used for ends both positive and negative. Practice with the methods in this book will give you control over the state, so that you can enter it at will to achieve goals you desire.

Have you ever been so involved in a movie, a book, a piece of music, a sports event, or a work project that you lost sight of your surroundings (for example, you didn't notice that the person you were with left to buy popcorn or go to the bathroom) and didn't notice the passage of time and were surprised to find that hours had passed? Have you ever gotten so caught up in a daydream — of falling in love, winning the Nobel Prize, or doing some great deed — that you had to spend a few seconds re-orienting yourself in time and space after you were interrupted?

If you've had any of these experiences, you have been in the focused state of attention that is a large part of mental training. These naturally occurring trances are common human experiences, by no means confined to situations where a person is meditating or involved with a hypnotist.

Most of the things we call fun can lead to trance. It's easy to become deeply involved in anything that feels good, and because of the involvement, it's just as easy to lose track of time and other matters. You may be deeply concerned about finances or health, but you forget about these things to the extent that you get engrossed in dance, games, a good movie, or something else you thoroughly enjoy.

Sex is one of the most common examples of everyday trance. When sex is good, the partners are strongly focused — on their own sensations or on what's happening to their mate — to the point that time is not noticed, noises are not heard, and even pain is not perceived or is less strongly perceived. A common example of the influence of trance in sex is when afterwards one partner tells the other about how much noise he or she has made and that partner is totally unaware of this. Another example is afterwards when you become aware of the pain of a bite or scratch. The pain would have been obvious to you when it was first created were you not so focused on your pleasure.

The antithesis of good sex is a lack of involvement, as, for instance, when one or both of the partners are not focused on what's happening but are standing back, watching, analyzing, and criticizing. A lack of involvement almost invariably leads to bad sex and sex therapists busily try to get clients more involved, more focused on sensation and feeling. All they are really trying to do is institute or re-institute the sharpened focus we are calling trance.

Orgasm is probably the ultimate trance. During the few seconds of orgasm, your attention is narrowed to a rather limited part of your being and it is almost impossible to think or be aware of other things. The physical sensations are so strong as to command your total involvement and attention. All other considerations are momentarily forced aside. And this, we think, is one of the main reasons that orgasm is so pleasurable.

While everyday trances are similar to mental training in

their inner focus, they differ in that they are not used systematically. Everyday trances are spontaneous happenings over which we generally exert little control. With a little help, however, we can use these events to great advantage.

Ironically, there is one kind of common experience that is often used systematically and with devastating results — what psychotherapist Daniel Araoz calls negative self-suggestion or negative self-hypnosis. The mind is never quiet, as those who have meditated know too well. It is always talking to itself, sending messages and images about all sorts of things. What hasn't been clearly recognized until recently is that a lot of what the mind says is negative: "You're too stupid to do well in this work," "You'll never be able to finish this task by the deadline," "You don't deserve anyone like him," "You'll never be happy." Negative self-suggestion is an automatic process in which people repeatedly tell themselves in words and images about their shortcomings and failures. People with low self-esteem, which includes most people suffering from depression, send almost continuous messages to themselves that they are stupid, inadequate, and incompetent, that everything will turn out badly, and that they deserve nothing better. Negative self-suggestion works. It is a self-fulfilling prophecy, bringing about in reality the inadequacy, worthlessness, and so forth that is imagined and suggested.

Take a depressed woman, for example, who continually tells herself that nothing will turn out well. On her way to a party, she tells herself over and over that there won't be anyone there worth meeting, that the whole event will be a bore, and that even if interesting people are present, they won't be interested in her. She enters the party with a cloud of gloom over her and makes real what was in her imagination. People tend not to want to meet her because she appears to be so negative, which, in fact, she is. She tends not to notice the interesting conversations going on around her and if she does notice that a certain man is attractive, she won't approach him (because she "knows" he wouldn't want to talk to her) and she sends out such negative messages that he's unlikely to approach her. So her despair is confirmed. She meets no one, does nothing, and leaves early because the party is so boring. "See," she tells herself on the way home, "life really is boring and depressing, not really worth living."

Many people, including a lot who believe that mental training doesn't work, are already masters at it, using their imaginations in negative ways and doing an incredibly effective job of making themselves miserable. Their unintentional use of informal, negative self-suggestion training follows the rules of effective mental training: it is done frequently and with great detail and involvement. They often are deeply engrossed, entranced, in their fantasized failures, inadequacies, and humiliations. And they usually have no idea of what this regular practice with negative thoughts and images is doing to them. In the therapeutic use of mental training, whether with a therapist or on one's own, the point is to use one's imagination in more constructive ways.

There are two main ingredients in effective mental training: *a relaxed, receptive state* and *positive suggestions*. We'll take them in reverse order and start with suggestions. The therapist or coach makes suggestions to the client to do or feel or be something different. When you do the process yourself, you make the suggestions to yourself. The suggestions can be about anything. Here are some examples: "Each time you practice mental training you will be more deeply and more fully relaxed, as relaxed and comfortable as you like"; "As you walk onto the stage to give your talk, you will experience the sensations in your stomach as signs of strength and confidence, giving you the energy to give an excellent presentation"; and "You will realize more and more each day that you are a worthwhile, lovable human being, deserving of respect and affection."

All mental training involves suggestions regarding behavior or feeling for the simple reason that the goal is to change behavior or feeling. Mental training can be looked at as *one* very powerful way to influence behavior.

The second feature of mental training has to do with receptivity to suggestion. Therapists talk about bypassing the critical faculty, of dealing with the right half of the brain, of talking to the subconscious. What they mean by these terms is simply receptivity to suggestion. They want to bypass the part of your mind that analyzes and criticizes, the part that says, for example, "There's no way you're going to be head of a department. You've never been in charge, never had the qualities needed to do the job. None of the management courses and books you've read has helped, and this imagery stuff won't either."

Relaxation is the most commonly used way to gain receptivity and a great deal of effort is put forth to help the client feel more comfortable and relaxed. A person comfortably relaxed in an easy chair is not likely to be critical. It's just so easy to listen and just go along, which is exactly what is wanted: acceptance of ideas rather than analysis or criticism of them.

Although relaxation is widely used, it is not the only way to foster greater receptivity. Paradoxical though it may seem, a heightened state of awareness — for example, repeatedly telling the client to feel more and be more aware of his or her energy — will accomplish the same result. But since relaxation is so easy for most people and is so commonly used in mental work, we will use it in most of our examples.

The term *trance* has many meanings, but can best be considered as that state of mind when a person is open to suggestion. Part of being receptive or in trance means a single-minded focus on an idea, a fantasy, or something else to the point that you become less aware of your surroundings. You are free to be aware if you want, but often it's easier not to be.

Meditation is one of the best-known ways to produce this focused state. Regardless of the type of meditation, the goal is a narrowed focus on a word, a phrase, a riddle, or something else. We view meditation as the first half of mental training. It produces the focused, receptive state we're interested in, but usually does not involve suggestion. When we work with people who have meditated and enjoyed it, we let them go into this state on their own, signaling when they're ready for us to give suggestions.

Let's look at mental training from a slightly different point of view. Some theorists talk about mental training as an altered state of consciousness, by which they mean a state of being that is somewhat different than the one we are usually in. In our everyday consciousness we are aware of many pieces of common reality — the time of day, our car and others around it as we drive, the people we're talking to, the stores or houses we pass as we walk, and so on. This has been called a generalized reality orientation. We are conscious of many parts of the external world in which we move. While we're in this mode, the rational part of our minds is active. It calculates whether we can risk driving faster on this stretch of road, how soon we'll reach our destination, if we have time to stop for a soda, or whether we're making the right impression on our customers or friends.

But there are other states of being where we're not as aware of external reality and where the rational faculty is less active. We have already mentioned a number of these: activities such as movie watching, book reading, sex, and fantasizing. To the extent that our attention narrows, that we get involved in what we are doing, and that we lose track of our external reality orientation, our state of consciousness is altered.

Of course it's not all-or-nothing. Our level of involvement in something, and therefore our state of consciousness, is really a continuum. For example, say you're busily at work answering letters and you think vaguely about paying a call on a customer the next day. You're basically alert, not much involved in the thought of calling on your customer, and you're aware of all the letters you have to go through before you can go home. This is your everyday consciousness. But say the thought of seeing this particular customer captures your attention for a moment. You recall him in greater detail and get a bit involved in what you might say when you call on him. For the moment you're doing this, you're losing contact with the time it now is and with the work you were doing. Your consciousness is not what it was a few minutes ago. You're experiencing what hypnotherapists call a light trance.

Say you get more deeply involved in your thoughts about the customer. You imagine yourself walking in the door, saying hello to several employees, saying such and such to the customer, being offered a cup of coffee, and so forth. You are probably totally unaware of the letters you're working on and the time of day. This is an example of medium trance.

Let's go further with our example. As you imagine being with your customer, you actually experience it in some ways. You feel his handshake, you taste the coffee, you feel the confidence or fear in your voice as you suggest a certain purchase, you hear his reply. You are very deeply involved, almost as if you were really there with the customer. You have no awareness that you are at your desk in your office with a pile of work in front of you and if you were asked, you not only wouldn't know the time but might not, without taking a moment to think about it, know what day it is. This is an example of deep trance.

The more involved you are, the deeper the trance, or the more altered your state of consciousness, the greater the effort to reorient yourself to external reality when you are interrupted. People in moderate to deep trance often act as if they were waking up from a sleep, moving and looking around to orient themselves in space and time.

To summarize, mental training is nothing extraordinary. All of us have the capacity to be receptive to suggestion, a state called trance, especially when we are relaxed and trusting. We see evidence of trance in much of our lives. We become so entranced at movies, at plays, in reading, and by our own fantasies that we forget where we are and actually feel as though we're there with Captain Kidd or chasing the great white whale or winning the man or woman of our fantasies. Such experiences can be thought of as altered states of consciousness.

Many of us also spend lots of time and energy giving ourselves negative suggestions about what we don't deserve and how badly things will turn out. The effectiveness of negative suggestion in bringing about negative results is powerful testimony to the strength of mental training. Imagine negative outcomes often enough and negative outcomes is what you'll get. The good news is that positive suggestion also works. Imagine positive outcomes often enough in a receptive state, and what you imagine will tend to be what you get. The therapeutic use of mental training lies precisely in using positive suggestions to the best effect.

But what, you want to know, is the point of getting relaxed and using the imagination? We've already answered this at the most general level: regular practice with relaxed positive imagery produces the kinds of changes you desire. It can help promote healing from physical injuries, illness, and surgery; mitigate pain from various ailments and medical and dental procedures; help women give birth more easily and more comfortably; improve study habits and test scores; enhance performance in almost all areas; and even help us in our relations with others.

We really aren't sure of all the ways mental training works, but we know a few things. We've already mentioned that a certain type of imagery produces changes in the way you perceive yourself and the world perceives you. If you imagine yourself a winner often enough, you'll start to act like one and be treated as one. Another thing we know is that the simple relaxation generated by deep breathing and by certain kinds of fantasies is itself extremely beneficial to good performance, whether we're talking about business productivity, athletic competition, sex, or just listening to other people.

Still another thing we know is that when you imagine yourself doing something — running a race, giving a talk, or whatever — the muscles respond to the imagery and actually do some of what you imagine them to be doing. If you watch skiers and bobsled teams do their visualizing before their events, you will see that their bodies actually move, directed only by their imaginations. You can program yourself mentally and physiologically to run the race the way you want, to give the talk the way you'd like, and so on. It's no wonder that so many athletes imagine themselves performing the way they want to perform. By using their imaginations, they are preparing themselves to perform in reality just as they imagine it in their minds.

These thoughts are summarized by scientist Elmer Green, who has studied voluntary control of bodily functions. "As we begin to realize that we are not totally the victims of our genetics, conditioning, and accidents, changes begin to happen in our lives, nature begins to respond to us in a new way, and the things that we visualize begin to happen with increasing frequency. Our bodies tend to do what they are told to do, if we know how to tell them." And how do we tell them? Not by issuing commands, not by force, says Green: "It is done by imagining and visualizing the intended change while in a relaxed state."

There's another important reason for relaxing and using your mind: it feels good. Most people who've used mental training say it is refreshing, comforting, and well worth the time. Some people go further, saying it feels exhilarating to use their minds in new ways, to learn new ways of being, and to get in touch with inner resources they barely knew they had.

Mental training consists of a large number of techniques, often bewildering in variety to professionals and laypersons alike. To introduce some order to the subject, we have divided the techniques of mental training into three categories: trance induction, uncovering techniques, and a group of methods designed to develop new habits and new ways of looking at yourself.

• *Trance induction.* Evoking or inducing trance usually involves some kind of relaxation. People help themselves to relax by taking deep breaths, by imagining peaceful scenes, by focusing on a phrase or word (as in meditation), or in a number of other ways. Although there are many standard inductions, anything that helps the person relax and turn inward is fine. The rigmarole of stage hypnotists and other entertainers — swinging pendulums, strident commands to go to sleep — is unnecessary and wasteful as well. Those who already know how to focus and relax, for instance because of experience with meditation, biofeedback, the techniques of natural childbirth, or some other relaxation method, should use the skills they possess.

• *Uncovering techniques.* These are used to discover the causes of problems — why, for instance, this woman never is able to complete a job or this man is unable to speak up in meetings. The names of some of these methods are affect bridge, age regression, and ideomotor signaling, but there's no reason for you to know them. Because uncovering methods work best when done with a therapist or guide, we do not deal with them in this book. Most readers will do fine without them.

• *A group of powerful methods whose purpose is to help you feel better about yourself and to develop new behaviors and feelings.* These methods can be used as well on your own as with the aid of a teacher, and they constitute the bulk of our book. We call these techniques changing the perspective and structure of your imagery, recalling past successes, imagining the results, imagining the process, positive self-talk, and posthypnotic suggestion.

You've encountered mental training or elements of it in places other than the examples of everyday trance we gave earlier. Many people who've been in psychotherapy, for instance, have probably experienced mental training or something very close to it, but usually without the label.

In traditional psychoanalysis, the patient lies on a couch and is instructed to say whatever comes to mind (free association). Lying down with the therapist out of view is certainly conducive to relaxation, and the suggestion to free-associate can be conducive to imaginary involvement, provided the patient does not try too much to analyze what she (or he) is saying. If the patient starts talking about an event and gets deeply into it, we could say she is in a trance. If, on the other hand, she tries to make sense of every statement and understand its meaning, the analytic side of her mind is too active and we don't have a good trance. Assuming she is in some kind of trance and the analyst makes an interpretation such as, "Now that you have relived that experience and can see how it's led to your present difficulties with finding a suitable relationship, you won't be bothered by that problem anymore," we in effect have a powerful posthypnotic suggestion, a subject about which we say lots more in chapter 11.

At the other extreme of therapeutic schools, behavior therapy makes extensive use of imagery and mental training, although the terms are rarely used. It is quite common for behavior therapists to ask patients to relax and then imagine being more assertive or being comfortable while undertaking a previously difficult task. Behavior therapists and sex therapists frequently use an approach called systematic desensitization, in which a graduated list of fearful scenes is presented to patients in a relaxed state. This is mental training pure and simple — basically a mixture of process imagery and goal imagery — and has been highly effective in resolving phobias and other difficulties.

Other therapies such as Gestalt and psychosynthesis make explicit use of imagery. The same is true of mass or pop therapies such as Silva Mind Control and Est, where the methods are sometimes carried to ridiculous extremes. A lot of Mind Control derives from the work of Emile Coue, whose main work was entitled *Self-Mastery through Conscious Autosuggestion*. Est also uses a number of standard hypnotic exercises. For example, the Est suggestion to "go into your space" is taken from hypnotic suggestions to find or create a safe place, a refuge, or a room of your own.

Management and sales courses use a great many mental-training techniques, although the term *mental training* is almost never mentioned. Much of the work in these courses derives from the thinking of people like Norman Vincent Peale and Maxwell Maltz, both of whom used hypnotic techniques. Course attendees are asked to imagine handling this or that situation in this or that way, to imagine feeling confident and relaxed when approaching a customer, to imagine fulfilling sales or production quotas.

The point of this brief survey is simply to demonstrate that you already know, from personal experience and perhaps also from courses and therapy, a lot about mental training. Trance, suggestion, visualization, mental training — call it what you will — is everywhere.

Fundamentally, mental training is simply a way to help you make better use of natural human abilities. We seek only to help you make better use of what you already have but either don't know you have or don't know how to use to best effect.

Many people lack confidence, but feeling confident is natural to human beings. Look at children learning to walk. They fall and fall, yet it seems clear that they all feel confident they will learn to walk without falling. Because of this feeling, they keep trying and sooner or later succeed in walking without falling. Almost all human beings have had at least one experience where they felt confident. It may have been years ago and it may not be remembered now, but it's there. It is very helpful for them to recall that experience and the attendant feelings. We call this technique recalling past successes and say more about it later. Done properly and repetitively, it can help people feel more confident in the present.

Likewise, everyone has had at least one experience of being more productive, more decisive, more assertive than usual. Helping a person reexperience that event and the accompanying feelings, and then applying those feelings to a current or future event, can make a huge difference. With writers suffering from writer's block, for example, it is beneficial to help them remember how good, powerful, and confident they felt when they were writing easily and well. Then we have them bring those feelings into the present. We tell them to imagine having those same feelings as they sit down at their desk tomorrow. All we are doing is reminding them of the good feelings they've had and the good writing they've done, and helping them apply the feelings to the present.

Nothing mystical, nothing magical, nothing out of the ordinary. Mental training is just using your innate abilities to best advantage.

The debt we owe to the play of imagination is incalculable.

— *Carl Gustav Jung*

CHAPTER 3

WHAT MENTAL TRAINING ISN'T

Despite the widespread positive publicity given mental training by athletes in recent years, there are still many misconceptions about its nature and uses. This is unfortunate: it means that some people who might benefit from using their minds in different ways won't do so because of their misunderstandings about what's involved. We hope to dispel ten of the more common myths. This chapter really constitutes a continuation of the previous one, because in discussing myths about mental training, we also elaborate on what it is.

Myth 1: Nothing This Simple and Easy Could Do Much Good

The idea here is that anything this simple must not be worth much. Criticisms like this often come from therapists who use analytic therapies that last many years and from people who've been in — or, more likely, are still in — such treatments. They think that mental training is just too superficial, too simpleminded, and that it doesn't get to the roots of the problems.

Our response is that although the techniques are simple and easy to learn and use, there's nothing simpleminded about them. They are based on sound knowledge of how the mind works and are consistent with recent research in psychology and the workings of the brain.

And there is no shortage of evidence that something this simple and easy really works. There are the statements of literally thousands of successful athletes, business people, professionals, and others who attribute much of their effectiveness to the disciplined use of the powers of the mind. To be sure, testimonials do not constitute scientific evidence. Yet it is sheer folly to disregard such a mountain of claims, especially since they are in basic agreement with each other and there is no contrary evidence.

There is also a lot of scientific support for the effects of mental training. Both in clinical and laboratory studies, mental training has been shown to produce reliable effects — for example, on the perception of pain, on bodily processes, and on increased performance — and to have excellent therapeutic effects with many common problems. Moreover, plenty of evidence exists that one of the major components of mental training as we teach it — relaxation — is by itself of great value both physiologically and psychologically. It's true that we aren't sure how all the effects of mental training are produced, but that in itself means little. Knowing that something has effects and understanding how the effects are produced are separate issues.

Although there is an abundance of evidence, increasing almost daily, as to the salutary effects of mental training, we should mention here that the techniques we describe in the second section of the book are not intended as one-shot cures. They are coping skills, if you like, or ways of training. They have to be used consistently, just as jogging, weight training, or writing has to be done consistently. Jack Nicklaus, for instance, still uses mental imagery before he sets up to hit a golf ball, just as he's been doing for over two decades.

Myth 2: Mental Training Is Only Positive Thinking

This myth is related to the first one. Especially in certain intellectual circles, there's a very strong bias against positive thinking. It is held to be a simpleminded refusal to face the harsh realities of life.

It is certainly true that mental training is loaded with positive thinking and positive imagery. That part is not a myth; but the unstated implication that positive thinking is useless is definitely wrongheaded. Positive thinking works. The more you think in terms of strengths, assets, and achievement of goals, the more you are likely to feel strong and confident, and to achieve your goals. Charles Garfield, who has studied thousands of high achievers in all fields, says that "peak performers distinguish themselves from those who merely do well by having a particularly strong expectation of success." In short, they think positively. Coaches, teachers, business people and their consultants all agree on one point: you've got to believe in yourself and your ability to realize your goals.

Positive thinking also works in a more prosaic way. Take the case of depression. It makes sense that someone who is poor, with no prospects for a good job, and who is having family problems, should be depressed; the situation is very depressing. But we find that a great many depressives are not in this situation at all. Many of them have good jobs, enough money, and even decent relationships. In fact, their situation is no different from most people who are not depressed. Research in recent years has yielded clear evidence that many depressives are the way they are precisely because they do not focus on the positive. Rather, they focus on what is negative or what might possibly become negative. They are using their minds to keep them down, whereas many other people, including a number of those whose reality is not half as good, feel better because they are using their minds to focus on what is good. Positive thinking is not only useful in attaining peak performance, it also seems necessary in keeping you sane.

We disagree that a positive attitude is simplistic. It is, on the contrary, solidly based on reality. We don't, for instance, overlook or deny the fact that a certain woman has cerebral palsy. She indeed does have it and that places certain restrictions on her. She is not going to become a champion runner no matter how much she practices and no matter how much imagery work she does. She may also not be a great dancer. But unlike many therapists, we aren't going to allow her to spend years or even months discussing or crying about her impairment. She has cerebral palsy, she has some limitations. That's sad, but what does she want to do with her life? We want to focus on what she can do and what she wants to do. People with cerebral palsy and other physical disabilities have accomplished great things and achieved great satisfaction. That's what we want to help her do. That's not simplistic positive thinking; it's positive thinking leading to achievable goals.

Consider a man who says of himself that he's quite ordinary, "really not very bright," doesn't understand economics, math, or physics, and is "not a business man." Not very encouraging and we probably wouldn't expect much of him. If he went into psychotherapy, a long time might be spent figuring out why he's so ignorant of math, physics, business, and economics. But this man did "have a knack for coining little phrases" and also for drawing. That's something to work with, though maybe not enough to get excited about. But Charles Schulz became obsessed with those knacks. He achieved fame and fortune beyond most people's dreams, and in the process enriched the lives of millions by putting those little phrases in the mouths of Charlie Brown, Lucy, and Snoopy.

Failures, mistakes, and defeats come to all of us. Happy and successful people don't dwell on these things but instead find ways of turning them to their advantage. We try to incorporate this pattern into our work. In 1978, Lee Iacocca was fired as president of Ford Motor Company. He had enough money to spend the rest of his life focusing on his misfortune and making himself miserable. He did sulk for a few days, but then he started thinking positively about what he wanted to do with his life and how to accomplish it. The rest is well known. He became president of Chrysler, a failing company, and took it to its greatest heights, in the process becoming richer and more famous than ever before. Chrysler was a mess when he took over and was close to financial ruin. Iacocca did not deny or disregard the harsh facts. He had to take them into account and did. But he also never lost faith that he would succeed. If what he did was simplistic positive thinking, we think the world could use a lot more of it.

The kind of positive thinking we and others employ in mental training does not deny reality, but it does focus on certain aspects of it instead of others. We acknowledge problems and limitations, but then quickly move on to focus on what can be done. This is similar to what Warren Bennis and Burt Nanus found in their study of leaders of American business: "For the most part, the leaders emphasized their strengths and tended to softpedal or minimize their weaknesses. Which is not to say that they weren't aware of personal weaknesses but rather that they didn't harp on them." Positive thinking, certainly. Simplistic, hardly.

Myth 3: What Counts Is Action, Not Fantasizing

Some people think that mental training means only training the mind and not doing anything else. One of our readers, who acknowledged at the outset that "I'm not into all this mental stuff," announced this after looking at an early version of some of our material: "Come on, Bernie, you know that what's important is doing, not fantasizing about it!" Her notion that mental training is nothing but using imagery couldn't be more wrong. But the issue is more complex than it first appears and requires some discussion.

Sometimes mental training by itself does work, To go back to the depressed people we mentioned a few pages back, what many of them need is not more accomplishments or more praise, but rather a different way of looking at their situation and themselves. One big problem is that they're perfectionists and tend to look at what they did wrong rather than what they did right, at the mistakes they made rather than the goals they realized, and at what they lack rather than what they have. The man with $5 million who is obsessively striving for another million is not going to feel better when he has it. He'll simply realize he doesn't have $10 million and obsessively go after that.

Helping these people requires getting them, dare we say it, to think more positively about themselves. They have to decrease the volume of self-critical thoughts and images they're producing and increase the volume of positive, self-affirming thoughts and images. They need to understand and believe that they're good and worthwhile even though they've made mistakes, aren't perfect, and don't have $6 million dollars. And this is what mental training — as well as related programs such as Rational-Emotive Therapy, cognitive behavior therapy, and many others — seeks to do. In many of these cases, what's needed is not different behavior but a different understanding of the person's behavior and achievements.

There is another way in which mental training is helpful by itself. How we picture ourselves and what we say to ourselves determines to a great extent how we project ourselves to the world. If you imagine yourself as incompetent, you tend to give other people the same impression and they act accordingly; for example, by not hiring or promoting you or by not going out with you. If you start imagining yourself as competent, on the other hand, you project this attitude and other people tend to act accordingly.

Having said that, we need to state emphatically that for most people mental training is not a substitute for action but rather a preparation for and an enhancement of it. Jack Nicklaus does not use mental training as a substitute for hitting golf balls — he would win very few games that way — but to help him hit the balls the way he wants. Arnold Schwarzenegger does not employ mental training instead of lifting weights but to increase the benefit of his weight lifting. Business people do not rely on goal imagery and process imagery instead of building plants and making products, but as a way of making their hard work more effective.

Mental training helps motivate and supply direction, often informs you of exactly what it is you need to do to realize your goals, and makes the work or practice more effective, but there is still lots of work to be done. In the majority of cases, mental training is just one part of a larger program to get what you want.

Myth 4: Only Special People
Can Benefit from Mental Training

We are often surprised by how many people who do believe in mental training think that only a small portion of highly gifted men and women can benefit from it. Those who make up this gifted elite, the story goes, have incredible powers of imagination and discipline, which must certainly be necessary to derive results from training the mind. It's almost as if these people are saying that you have to have a very special mind to benefit from training the mind. This misunderstanding probably owes something to a misconception about hypnosis (one of the terms for mental training): it has long been thought that only special people could make use of it.

There has been a rethinking of this issue among hypnotists in recent years. Current estimates are that the vast majority of men and women, probably 90 to 95 percent, can use hypnosis. If you can relax and imagine, you are a good candidate. If you have trouble relaxing and fantasizing, it is probable that you can learn to do both.

It is true that there are different degrees of hypnosis or mental training; that is, the extent to which someone gets involved in imagery can vary. It is also the case that different people have varying capacities for such involvement. Perhaps only 10 to 20 percent can get involved enough (or deeply enough, as it is often put) that they can have major surgery without chemical anesthesia. The good news is that for the vast majority of goals people wish to achieve, light involvement (or light trance, as hypnotists call it) is all that is required.

In discussing this myth, we came across a misconception about hypnosis that influences perceptions of mental training. The following myths have similar roots. They are the result of what people have learned about hypnosis, either through nightclub acts or the popular media. Before going on to them, we want to say that although hypnosis and mental training can be used synonymously, hypnosis as generally used by health professionals includes more than the mental training we teach. For instance, hypnosis includes a lot of work with the uncovering methods mentioned in chapter 1, whereas most people training the mind to enhance performance do not make much use of these techniques.

Myth 5: Hypnosis Must Be Dramatic to Be Effective

The common impression is that hypnosis is spectacular and strange. Hypnotized people supposedly look different: without expression and glassy-eyed, as if heavily drugged. And of course they behave in unusual ways, talking with slurred speech and walking like Frankenstein's monster.

The truth is that there is nothing strange or spectacular about hypnosis. The basic component is focused attention, usually accompanied by relaxation, hardly anything to get excited about. In light-to-medium states of hypnosis, the most common kind, people can and do talk, and usually not much differently than they usually talk. They also walk normally and do other acts in the usual way. Hypnosis is so unspectacular that most people who are hypnotized for the first time refuse to accept the fact of their hypnosis. The common response is, "I was very relaxed . . . but I didn't go under (or, didn't lose consciousness)."

Sometimes clients have beliefs based on the myth of hypnosis as high drama. Some time ago, we were consulted by a man who insisted that hypnosis required swinging a pendulum before his eyes and commanding him to go to sleep. We tried to explain that pendulums and commands were unnecessary, to no avail. Only when we put together a pendulum and swung it before him, simultaneously commanding him to go to sleep, did he become hypnotized.

This client put his finger on another aspect of the drama of hypnosis — the authoritarian stance of the hypnotist, who barks out commands like an officer in the SS. This also makes for great theater but has little to do with reality. Some therapeutic hypnotists are more forceful than others, but rarely do they make demands or bark orders. In many cases, the suggestions are given in such a way as to be barely noticeable. For example: ". . . and as you become more and more comfortable, you may find yourself wondering just how much more satisfaction you will feel when you've achieved your goal of returning to school."

As we discussed in the last chapter, hypnosis is a common human experience usually called by other names, such as daydreaming, fantasizing, and so on. Rarely is there anything dramatic about it. But often therapist or client, or both, decide high drama is required and proceed to put on a show, which may be entertaining but has nothing to do with hypnosis.

Speaking of entertainment, we need to say something about the height of silliness, hypnosis as presented in nightclubs and movies. All sorts of wondrous things are witnessed in stage hypnosis and almost none are what they seem to be. Stage hypnosis is an entertainment and far closer to show business than what is practiced by doctors, therapists, and athletic coaches. Since the main purpose is entertainment, any means, fair or foul, are seen as legitimate. One stage hypnotist writes that the "hypnotic show must be faked" and recommends that someone wanting to be a successful stage hypnotist "forget all about trying to be a legitimate hypnotist."

One method involves the hypnotist simply telling a

subject to do what is wanted — for example, to crow like a rooster. The subject, wanting to put on a good show and please the hypnotist, crows and the audience believes the performance is a consequence of hypnosis. The extent to which people will go to please the hypnotist is fascinating. They will fake it, they will lie. They will eat hot mustard and say it is delicious ice cream, even though the taste is horrible.

We have it on the authority of Mark Twain that they will even endure pain. As a boy, Twain volunteered to be a subject for a stage hypnotist and pretended to go into a deep trance. He even allowed people to stick needles through his flesh; the pain was excruciating (which would not be true had he been deeply hypnotized), but Twain suppressed all signs of it. The audience, which included Twain's mother, was impressed. Twain later told his mother the truth but she refused to believe him. After all, she had seen the needles go in without sign of pain and that was more convincing to her than his belated testimony to the contrary.

The most important requirement for a stage hypnotist is to select his volunteers carefully. Hypnotist/entertainers know from experience which members of the audience are most likely to play the game. Typically, a number of people are selected and then put through some quick tests by the hypnotist. Those who aren't as cooperative as wanted are quietly asked to leave, and only the most cooperative are left. The young Mark Twain was obviously a good choice because he would do anything to please the hypnotist.

Stage hypnotists also exploit widespread ignorance about the capacities of the human body. A favorite trick is to tell a presumably hypnotized subject that his body is becoming stiff and rigid. Once the subject looks stiff, he is placed between two chairs, one under his head, the other under his ankles. The subject becomes a human plank, suspended between the two chairs for several minutes. The more advanced version of this trick is to have a second person stand on the chest of a human plank with one chair under the shoulders and one chair under the calves. The audience believes that although hypnosis may be weird, it certainly gives extraordinary strength.

What the audience doesn't realize is that the plank trick has nothing to do with hypnosis. Studies have shown that the feat is within the normal abilities of many people, with or without hypnosis. Interestingly, the subjects in these experiments are usually surprised at their own accomplishment. We do not suggest, however, that you go out and try this. While many people are capable of it, there have also been reports of back and neck injuries.

Fire walking is another phenomenon that has strengthened the association in some people's minds between hypnosis and high drama. The claim has been made that under hypnosis you can walk without harm over very hot coals or stones. There are even workshops to prepare you for it. And sure enough, people walk through the coals without burns.

Dramatic it certainly is, but it has nothing to do with hypnosis. Almost anyone can walk without harm over hot coals as long as he or she keeps moving at a steady pace. If you stop, you will surely get burned. We do not encourage you to try this, especially on your own. Fire walking is best done socially with at least one person in attendance who has done it before.

As for movies, perhaps the less said, the better. Hollywood has never been known for its concern for accuracy. Hypnosis in the movies bears the same relationship to real hypnosis as the Old West of the Lone Ranger and Roy Rogers bears to the real Old West — which is to say, almost none. Altogether too many films depict the Evil Hypnotist putting the Good Guy under his spell and commanding him in trance (and what a trance!) to commit unspeakable acts. From scenes like this comes the myth that hypnosis is dangerous, that the subject is under the control of the hypnotist and can be made to do things he wouldn't otherwise do. We know hypnotherapists who can't even get some of their patients to pay their bills or come on time to appointments, so how is it that in the movies hypnotists can get people to sign over all their money to them or to kill their spouses?

Even though it is called hypnosis, what you see in nightclubs, in movies, and on many television programs is not legitimate hypnosis. It is magic and drama, designed to make you laugh and have a good time. There is nothing wrong with these ends as long as you don't confuse an entertainment with a powerful change technique.

Myth 6: Hypnotized People "Go Under" or Are "Put Under" and Have Amnesia about What Occurs

This idea assumes that hypnosis involves a loss of consciousness, that it is a kind of sleep. Clients are somehow "under" their everyday consciousness, whatever that might mean, and don't know what's going on.

It is certainly true that many people feel different in hypnosis than they do otherwise. If nothing else, they are more relaxed and more focused. But the metaphor is all wrong. What is it that they are under? A small number of people do fall asleep during hypnosis because the relaxation is conducive to sleep, especially if a person is tired. But hypnosis and sleep are physiologically separate entities. Sleep is sleep and ends the hypnosis. When the person awakens, it's a normal awakening.

It makes no sense that hypnotists would try to induce

loss of consciousness, because they want to influence people and, with rare exceptions, it is very difficult to influence someone who is unconscious or asleep.

The going-under-and-losing-consciousness business also makes no sense in view of the fact that hypnotized people are aware of as much as they want to be. They perceive extraneous sounds (traffic, conversations, doors opening and closing) and follow the therapist's voice if they want to. Interestingly, this awareness is often used by clients to deny being hypnotized ("I wasn't hypnotized, Doc, because I heard every word you said"). Of course people aren't aware of everything that occurs while in hypnosis, but this is a meaningless statement. No matter what state of consciousness we're in, we are not aware of everything that occurs. Our minds wander and we miss some things. A similar process occurs in hypnosis.

Do people under hypnosis experience amnesia? There are two types of amnesia to discuss, spontaneous and suggested. *Spontaneous amnesia* is forgetting hypnotic events without a suggestion to that effect from the hypnotist. Spontaneous amnesia is far from common. There are hypnotists who have practiced for years, using hypnosis many times each week, who have rarely experienced a case of spontaneous amnesia.

Occasionally a hypnotic patient or subject is amnesic, but even here it's important to keep things in perspective. People forget things all the time. In a large class, for example, there are always some students who can't remember anything that took place just a few minutes ago. And without any hypnosis at all, therapy clients sometimes can't remember anything about the last session. Hypnotic amnesia needs to be analyzed in this perspective.

Suggested amnesia is a different matter. It makes sense that a person who is deeply involved in hypnosis and following the suggestions of the hypnotist should be able to forget when asked to. However, as any beginner in hypnosis will be happy to tell you, amnesia is often difficult to bring about; the therapist may suggest it, command it, and beg for it, but it may not occur. If it does occur, it can break down at any time. Even with good hypnotic subjects and an experienced hypnotherapist, not everyone is amnesic when given suggestions not to remember.

But keep in mind that the fact of suggested amnesia does not support notions that the hypnotized person is "under" anything or "out of it." Rather, among men and women who follow hypnotic suggestions, some of them will also follow suggestions not to remember, particularly if the amnesia serves a useful purpose for them.

Myth 7: People Can Get Stuck in a Trance and Never Return to Reality

This misconception stems from the being-under and being-out-of-it ideas. Clients to whom hypnosis is offered often voice concern that they'll get lost in inner space and not be able to return.

There is absolutely no validity to this idea. There is no getting stuck somewhere because you're not going anywhere. There is no "there" to get stuck in. You're merely going to experience yourself in a way that is different from your ordinary waking consciousness — in a way you've experienced before in fantasies, when watching movies, and under other circumstances. The idea of getting stuck in hypnosis is as absurd as the notion that you might get stuck in a dream or fantasy and not be able to get out.

It is true that some hypnotized persons do not always "wake up" when the hypnotist says they should (a fact that in itself says something about their losing all power to the hypnotist). The reasons for this vary from wanting to continue with the pleasant experience they're having to not wanting to face a difficult situation in their lives. A number of times, we have had clients not "wake up" when we ask them to. Often they telegraph their intentions by shaking their heads when we say "your eyes will open and you'll be awake and alert." We usually then say something like, "Oh, seems like you want to continue as you are," to which they usually nod in agreement. And later they give their reasons.

Recently, a woman refused to "awaken" for a few minutes. When she opened her eyes, she said: "I was feeling better than I've felt in years. I just wanted to have that experience for a while longer." In every single case we have heard of, clients come back to ordinary consciousness within a few minutes. In experiments where the hypnotist stopped talking for a few minutes or left the room, subjects either fell asleep and later awoke as they usually do or else simply opened their eyes and were perfectly normal.

It is important to remember that even when clients momentarily resist the therapeutic suggestion to "wake up," they do so of their own volition. They choose to keep their eyes closed and continue with their experience. Rather than being stuck somewhere or having lost control, they are exercising their power to do what they want.

Myth 8: People under Hypnosis Surrender Control to the Hypnotist and Will Do Whatever They Are Told

This widespread notion, touched on earlier, holds that subjects somehow give up control to the hypnotist, who can get them to do anything at all, no matter how contrary to their values.

To keep this matter in perspective you have to remember that many people, under circumstances having nothing to do with hypnosis, will do almost anything requested of them. To take a common example, people often end up buying things — everything from deodorants to cars to computers — that they don't want or can't afford or have little use for, just because of advertisements or other sales pressure. In laboratory experiments having nothing to do with hypnosis, it has been demonstrated many times that research subjects are willing to harm animals or other people if the researcher pressures them even a little to do so. People are moved by many things — guilt, awe, respect, fear of being different — to commit acts they don't want to commit. We need not invoke a special state called hypnosis to account for this phenomenon.

There is no documented case of someone doing something contrary to his or her values because of hypnosis. If you want to get people to do something they don't want to do, you may well be able to persuade them to do it; it is doubtful that hypnosis would be of much help.

There are many examples of people *not* doing what the hypnotist wants. We have already mentioned several; for instance, not paying the hypnotist's bills and not being amnesic in accordance with suggestion. An even more common example concerns what subjects imagine when the hypnotist suggests a particular scene. We have often found, when talking to a client after a hypnotic session, that he or she imagined something other than what we suggested. To return to the image of lying on a warm beach, some clients say something like this: "I got nervous when you said to imagine the sun's rays warming me. As a child, I got horribly sunburned and suffered with blisters for days at a time. So I just pictured being in a shady meadow." If people aren't willing to imagine an ordinary scene that caused them discomfort in the past, it's unlikely they will imagine blowing up City Hall.

But suppose, the question always arises, a person is already very angry with the inhabitants of City Hall; couldn't hypnosis be used to get him to imagine blowing it up and then actually to do it? If so, it's because he's already imagined the scene by himself many times. But as far as carrying out the fantasy, the chances are probably no better with hypnosis than without.

Far from taking away control, hypnosis seeks just the opposite: to give you control in areas where you don't have it or more control in areas where you don't have as much as you want. It seeks to give you control over inherent abilities and skills, such as the ability to feel good about yourself, to speak confidently, to perform at your peak.

Myth 9: Hypnosis Endows People with Extraordinary Powers

Part of this myth derives from stage hypnosis where volunteers perform incredible feats such as the human-plank trick or presumably feel no pain when needles are stuck in them. Part of the myth comes from demonstrations of legitimate hypnosis where, for example, volunteers experience so-called positive and negative hallucinations, seeing what isn't there and not seeing what is there, and often have amnesia for the hypnotic experience.

While much of stage hypnosis is faked, the other phenomena are real. Many hypnotized subjects can see what isn't there and not see what is; and hypnosis is perhaps the most effective psychological method of pain control we have. And, as noted earlier, suggested amnesia works for some people. But there is nothing extraordinary about these things. We all have the capacity to ignore pain, to forget, to see things that aren't present and not to see things that are. If that statement sounds strange, hold on a minute and we'll explain what we mean.

We all see things that aren't there. For example, a couple goes shopping for a new home and as they inspect one that's promising, they see themselves in it. They imagine waking up in the bedroom, eating in the breakfast room, and so on. The Realtor doesn't see what they see and neither does anyone else. The couple is experiencing a positive hallucination. They are not actually eating or waking up in the new house; they are just imagining doing so. Smart salespeople are aware of the phenomenon and suggest images to get things moving — for example, "Can you imagine how pleasant it is to wake up in such a large and sunny room?"

Certain professions put a large premium on the ability to see what isn't there. Architects, for instance, have to be able to visualize what the living room will look like if that wall is removed and this one is pushed back three feet. Interior designers have to be able to visualize what the same room will look like if such and such a lighting scheme is used and with such and such furniture and decorations. Engineers have to imagine how a bridge or plane not yet built will look. The ability to see what isn't there is inherent to human beings. Hypnosis is simply a way of getting in better touch with it and gaining some control over it.

As for not seeing what is there, we do it all the time. How many times have you looked for your keys, glasses, or another object when all the time it was right in front of you? There's nothing strange or unusual about the phenomenon. Forgetting where things are is very similar to not seeing what is there. Most of us have had the experience of walking down the street and suddenly being grabbed by someone we know who says, "I thought you were going to walk right by me. You didn't even notice me." Yet there they were, right in front of you. But your attention was elsewhere and you literally didn't see what was in front of you. The ability not to see or hear or feel something is deeply rooted in human beings.

Not noticing pain sounds like a trickier subject, but it isn't. The perception of pain is blunted to the extent that we are distracted. If your mind is elsewhere, the sensations that cause pain don't hurt, or don't hurt as much. Recently we were watching a little girl jumping off a sofa. She was having a great time of it until she landed on her head and started howling with pain. Obviously it hurt. But she returned to her game in a few minutes and once again hit her head, exactly as before. But this time, before she could cry, we distracted her with loud noises and funny faces. She got into the spirit of things and started making faces at us. She did not cry or seem to be in pain. The best explanation seems to be that she got engrossed in the game to the extent that she never experienced the pain. Many parents know about this principle and immediately offer distractions of various sorts when a child is hurt.

What is true of children is also true of adults. We've all had experiences where we were in pain but didn't notice it while we were involved in something else. Clearly, we are born with abilities to be immune or at least relatively insensitive to pain. Exactly how these abilities operate is not known, but we do know that they can be more fully developed by mental training.

Hypnosis really doesn't seek to add anything to the person. Rather, it seeks to use capacities we all have, to make us more aware of them, and to give us the ability to develop and use them so that we can achieve goals that are healthy and beneficial. The only thing extraordinary about it is that most of the time most people don't use abilities they already possess.

Myth 10: Hypnosis Is a Panacea

There are people who have made claims that hypnosis and other kinds of mental training can cure cancer, take people back to past lives, and be used like a lie detector in criminal investigations to get people to speak the truth.

Aside from chicken soup, there are no panaceas. The methods of hypnosis and mental training are not effective with every person or with every problem. Like all other methods in all fields, they have their sphere of applicability, places where they work very well, and they also have limits. We have several times mentioned areas where mental training has demonstrated its usefulness. But we have no satisfactory evidence that it can cure cancer or get witnesses in courtrooms to speak the truth.

Since past-lives regression has attracted so much attention in recent years and turned off so many people to hypnosis, we should say a few words about it. Most therapists with a lot of experience using hypnosis have had a few patients say that they went back to previous lives. That is a fact. What you do with that fact is another matter.

The imagination by definition is different from everyday rational consciousness. As in fantasy and dreams, it allows a different type of perception and consciousness than is usually present. Since the imagination is not limited by the ordinary constraints of time and space, it allows us to imagine things as we wish they were or, negatively, as we fear they might be. It allows us to change the past and prepare for the future. These qualities are necessary for mental training to work. Imagining yourself being different will help you to be different. But having an image of yourself as the queen of England will not make you into the queen, any more than dreaming of great wealth will automatically change the size of your bank account.

The problem with past-lives regression is that some therapists have taken fantasy productions literally, assuming that if patients report being alive during the French Revolution, they must indeed have been alive at that time. This conclusion is not justified by the facts. We have no idea of what fantasy productions such as age-regression mean, except that they are often helpful to those who have them. Many people — whether with hypnosis, psychoanalysis, or something else — do in one way or another "go back" to a time when they were younger, recall certain events, and feel better as a result. But this says nothing about the validity of what is recalled or experienced. There is plenty of evidence that what people recall — in hypnosis, psychoanalysis, courtrooms, and elsewhere — is not always true, even when they feel certain that it is.

Past-lives stories have also been subjected to some scrutiny. Without getting into the details here, we'll just say that these stories tend to break down under close examination. Research has indicated that subjects are suggestible and will tend to produce the kind of material wanted by the experimenters and therapists.

The notion that visualizing a parking space will automatically produce one has also caused confusion about what the mind can do. Some people who practice this kind of imagery assume that there is something magical about it, that their imagery somehow influences someone who's taking up a parking place to leave at the precise time they want to move into that spot. We suggest that if people really had this kind of power, they could use it more profitably at a crap table or in a state lottery, and hire a chauffeur to find parking places for them.

Imagining a parking space may help you find one, but not because of anything magical. It helps the same way any kind of imagery helps, by mobilizing the powers of your mind to achieve a desired state — in this case, by making you more alert and more aware of the possibilities. If you imagine a parking place of the exact dimensions your car requires, you may realize that the little space across the street will do, and thus may see what you otherwise might have overlooked. The activity of your mind may also give you a different perspective — for instance, an awareness that some pedestrians are walking toward their parked cars. With this understanding, you will observe more closely and perhaps ask them if they're going to move their cars.

With or without imagery, sooner or later everyone finds a parking place, even in crowded cities. But that doesn't necessarily prove you are possessed of superhuman powers or that mental imagery is a panacea.

We do not apologize for the limits of mental training. Its sphere of applicability is very broad and it is very good in those areas. These are the things for which it should be used. Mental training is not magic, and although it sometimes produces spectacular results, this is not the norm. Mental training is simply a very useful tool; like all tools, it needs to be used with care and common sense. It probably can't make you into a superman or superwoman, but it can do a lot to improve the ways you handle almost everything you do.

It is not enough to have a good mind. The main thing is to use it well.

— *René Descartes*

CHAPTER 4

SETTING YOUR GOALS

The rest of this book consists of suggestions and exercises to help you use mental training for whatever constructive and desirable goals you have. Most people can be their own experts, using this book as a guide. As we've said before, there is nothing strange or artificial about mental training. Aside from a few small things such as the book and a tape recorder, you have all the essential equipment within you — a mind and the abilities to relax and to imagine. Even hypnotists, who sometimes engage in a lot of theatrical mumbo jumbo, at least in part designed to inflate their importance, admit that all hypnosis is really self-hypnosis. The hypnotist only guides you. Although there are a few mental-training techniques best done under the guidance of an expert — those called uncovering techniques, designed to discover the sources of problems, as mentioned earlier — everything else in mental training can be done by yourself. The remainder of the book will provide you with the knowledge you need to use mental training for your own purposes.

Some people find this difficult to believe and ask if it isn't advisable to have a consultant or therapist. You may, of course, need to get information from other sources. Depending upon your goals, you may want to take courses, read other books, or get consultation to pick up information and skills. But what you need to know about the methods of mental training can be gotten simply by applying what is in the following chapters. If you find that you have trouble understanding the methods or putting them into practice, or that you're not achieving the desired results, you may want to consider ordering the prerecorded audio tapes we've prepared (see the last page of this book).

When meditation was in vogue in the 1960s and 1970s, its most successful school, Transcendental Meditation, popularized the notion that a special course was needed because in that course a unique and personal mantra — a phrase to be meditated on — would be given to each student. The implication was that without the course and the special mantra, meditation would be less effective. This, of course, was a marketing ploy. The folks at TM wanted people to pay money to take their course rather than to learn meditation from a friend or a book.

The research of Harvard physician Herbert Benson and others clearly demonstrated that what is important about meditation can be learned in a few moments from a book or lecture. The essential result of meditation, what Benson calls the relaxation response and what we call trance, can be achieved by anything that promotes relaxation and receptivity. As for special mantras, Benson demonstrated that there is no need for them. The important thing is the act of focusing, not what is focused upon. Benson suggests focusing on the number one or any word or phrase that you like. Doing so produces the same response as focusing on so-called special mantras.

Keep in mind that you've already been in the required receptive state, trance, many times, probably hundreds or even thousands of times. The problem is that you don't know how you do it and don't have any control over the process. We're going to give you that control so that you can use mental training to achieve your goals.

You may also want to keep in mind that many people have stumbled onto these techniques on their own and use them to their benefit with no training of any kind. This was the case with many of the high achievers in American business and sports studied by Charles Garfield; a number of those who used mental-training techniques didn't even know there were names for them. The chances are excellent you won't need any more than the suggestions we give. If you're already using some of the methods we present, allow our suggestions to help you use them more effectively.

One important and wonderful thing about mental training you should know is that it can easily complement any other work you are doing to achieve your goals. It is not inconsistent with any form of management or sales training, athletic or artistic training, education, or psychotherapy we know of. Use what we present to get the most out of your other efforts.

We've mentioned goals a number of times and now it's important to get down to cases. If you're going to use mental training to help you achieve the results you want, you first have to decide what those results are.

Setting proper goals is a large part of the battle to achieve them. Many people set goals in such a way that they're impossible to accomplish or such that it's impossible to determine whether or not they were accomplished. "I want to be more effective," "I want to get along better with others," and "I want to be happier" are all examples of overly general statements. They are too vague to give direction or incentive, and too vague for you to determine if and when they've been achieved.

It is also true that many times people have no idea why they're doing what they're doing. We know how strange this sounds, but it's true at every level and in every field. We've seen it among professionals, among athletes, among business people. We've even seen it among workaholics; they work for days, weeks, and months on end, with no idea of what they're trying to accomplish. They remind us of the people described by the philosopher George Santayana as "redoubling their efforts after losing sight of the objective." We believe that one of the main reasons that people fail in using self-help materials, in psychotherapy, and in many other areas of life is because of a lack of clear-cut goals. We also believe that one reason so many high-school and college students have so much trouble focusing on their studies is because they don't have a goal, don't know what all this studying is leading to.

The damage done by not having a goal is frequently seen in writing and public speaking. When a letter, article, or talk seems to wander aimlessly, chances are good the author or speaker never was clear about what he was trying to do. One way we help writers and speakers is to demand a clear statement of what they want to convey with a particular talk or piece of writing. It's amazing how many look puzzled and say, "Gee, I'm not sure."

Having objectives and keeping sight of them is crucial. This idea was well expressed by the great football coach Vince Lombardi, when asked by John Madden what separated good coaches from bad coaches: "The best coaches know what the end result looks like, whether it's an offensive play, a defensive coverage, or just some area of organization. If you don't know what the end result is supposed to look like, you can't get there." Madden learned his lesson well. "After that," he has written, "whenever I put something new in the Raider playbook, I always tried to picture what the end result should look like. And then I worked to create that result."

You can't get there if you don't know where you're going. Setting goals gives direction; it tells you what to do and where to go, making decisions much simpler. It also makes what you're doing more satisfying. When the work gets tedious or arduous, as it will at times, knowledge of the goal makes it worthwhile. Having a goal in mind supplies incentive, something always needed.

Proper goal setting is an art in itself, one that successful people generally are very good at. Goal setting is also more complicated than it seems. There are long-range goals and short-range goals, and there is also something else we call mission that we'll get into a bit later.

Before you get started with the exercises in the following chapters, it is in your interest to spend some time establishing the goals you desire to reach. This chapter will help you do that.

Your long-range goal is what you ultimately want to accomplish. We are, however, being a bit loose with our use of *ultimate* and *long-term*. These terms don't necessarily mean your ultimate goal in life or your goals for twenty years hence. They simply refer to a goal that is important for you to achieve. There may be many short-range goals, all of which are stepping-stones or means to the ultimate goal. Both long- and short-range goals should be as specific as possible. The more specific they are, the better your chances of realizing them. If you have trouble being specific and keep coming up with generalities such as wanting to be happier or more productive, ask yourself what it would take to make you happier or more productive; conversely, ask yourself how you would know when the goals had been achieved. Chances are good that the answers to these questions will be reasonably specific goals to aim for. If, for instance, you say that you'd feel happier if you were making $30,000 more a year, you may want to make that your goal. If you know you'd be more productive if you turned out twenty pages or forms or whatever a day, then that's your goal.

Before you get to work on your goals, we want to explain the idea of *mission*. A mission or purpose is the reason for your ultimate goal, the why of what you want. Wanting to prove you're as good as or better than other people in some specific way, wanting to reach a certain level of financial security, wanting to be the best writer there is or the fastest runner or the best cabinetmaker, wanting to use more of your potential, wanting to be in the best possible health, wanting to help your company, family, or neighborhood achieve a certain goal — all these are examples of missions. They are too general to serve as goals, but are extremely important nonetheless. Often a mission is what provides the motivation to accomplish goals. Of course we already said that the ultimate goal provides motivation for accomplishing short-range goals. There's no contradiction. Motivation is often hard to come by, especially when the going gets tough, and the more sources of motivation you have pushing you forward, the better off you'll be. So let thoughts of the ultimate goal fuel your pursuit when they can, and let the same be true for thoughts of your mission.

The goal of this chapter is to help you come up with a written statement consisting of three elements: your *ultimate goal,* your *mission,* and one or more *short-range goals.* We suggest you go through the process described below even if you believe you already know what your goals are. You may change your mind about what goals to pursue or perhaps focus more specifically on what you want. If not, you haven't lost much.

Here are some examples of what the finished product might look like.

Ultimate Goal
To own my own travel agency

Mission
1. To be the first woman in my family to have her own business
2. *To be the boss;* to work only for myself, so I can set my own schedule and rules

Short-Range Goals
1. Complete course at university in running a small business
2. Set up networks to get referrals
3. Get financial consultation re best way to set up business
4. Arrange for loans
5. Rent office
6. Keep working on ads I'll use when office is opened

The above plan was set up by one of our clients several years ago. The project took two years to completion and was successful. When the going got rough, as it did because she had grave doubts about her ability to do all this on her own, thinking about being the boss (her emphasized phrase) and being the first woman business owner in her family helped push her along. This was a woman with very little business experience except for a job as a travel agent. She came from a family where a successful woman was one who worked part-time as a clerk or secretary to supplement her husband's earnings. She had difficulties with all of her goals and had to do a lot of imagery and other work to achieve them. Even renting an office was difficult for her; the only things she had rented previously were two apartments, one when she was a student and one when she left school. But she worked hard, using her imagery every day and doing the other things that were required, and ended up with what she desired.

Ultimate Goal
To get in better physical condition, as I was three years ago (at the very least, this would mean losing 25 pounds and being able to walk up the steps to my apartment without being winded)

Mission
1. To give my body the care and respect it deserves
2. To feel better about myself

Short-Range Goals
1. Talk to Dr. Jones about a sensible diet to replace the crash ones I've been using
2. Tuna sandwich and salad instead of pizza and beer dinners on Fridays
3. Talk to Janet [his girlfriend] about helping me stay on diet
4. Make time for exercise
5. Jog a mile (working up to 3 miles) every Tues., Thurs., and Sat. evening; do weights on Mon. and Wed. evenings
6. Whenever possible, walk to work instead of taking car
7. Talk to Janet about doing more walking on our outings

The preceding statement is more detailed than others we've seen, in that it includes things some people wouldn't think necessary — for example, finding time for exercise. But it worked very well for this man and there are lessons to be learned from him. Many people plan to do something such as exercise without realizing there's no time for it given the way their lives are structured. They often end up exercising sporadically, only when they happen to have free time, and thus do not achieve their goals. It's an excellent idea to plan ahead and make time for the new things you decide to do, which often means curtailing other activities. That way, you don't have to search around every day for time; it has been planned for and is available for you.

Ultimate Goal
To get at least a 3.4 grade point average this year

Mission
To ensure that I can get into one of the better grad schools

Short-Range Goals
1. Arrange for tutors for statistics and Russian
2. Take course at Health Center on reducing test-taking anxiety
3. Spend four hours of uninterrupted time studying on M, T, and F, and six hours on W and Th
4. Quit Photography Club to make more time for studying

This program is typical of that used by a number of students with whom we've worked. Our experience is that those students willing to plan such a program and carry it out with the help of mental training significantly improve their grades.

Ultimate Goal
To feel more comfortable around women, so I could approach one at work or at a party without sweating and feeling jittery, start a conversation, and ask for a date if I want to

Mission
1. To overcome my lifelong shyness around women (which would make me feel terrific)
2. To find a good, lasting relationship

Short-Range Goals
1. Ask Jean [his sister] how women like to be approached and what they're looking for
2. Read [Philip] Zimbardo's book on *Shyness*
3. Chat more with Sylvia [a secretary at work] and Jane [a colleague] to see if I can feel more comfortable with them
4. If #3 works out, ask them same questions I asked Jean
5. Invite Jan [a neighbor he felt reasonably comfortable with but was not romantically attracted to] to lunch at my place and ask her to bring her friend Alicia [whom he had met once briefly and found attractive]

This may sound like a man in his early teens or twenties, but in fact he was forty-two. There are many shy men around, of all ages. There are also many shy women, but because, even in these liberated times, the burden for social and sexual initiation is still very much on men, they're the ones who suffer the most from shyness. A shy woman may still get asked out, but a shy man has a far smaller chance. This man's program was a good start to overcoming his problem. Talking to his sister and women at work did help him feel a little more comfortable, as did reading the book he listed. The fifth short-range goal was far more difficult and required a lot of mental training as preparation. Alicia came to the lunch, which went well, but it turned out she was involved with someone. But the man used the opportunity to try out his new skills in talking to women he didn't know. He then had to add new short-range goals to his program, which included starting conversations with women in the grocery store he frequented and at parties.

Goals can be much simpler than in the four examples above. Sometimes they are mainly one-shot efforts. For example, a woman might like to ask a certain man for a date but have difficulty mustering up the courage. Her goal would be simply to ask him out. It's possible in a case like this that she needn't come up with a mission or any means short of rehearsing in her mind how she's going to approach him. If this mental rehearsal provides the needed impetus, she's achieved her goal. If it doesn't suffice, however, she may have to do more; for example, she may want to do more relaxation work combined with imagining herself being more assertive with a variety of people, only gradually working her way up to asking this man out. Other examples of one-shot goals include asking the boss for a raise, asking the neighbors to keep their stereo down, or participating in a new activity just once for the experience (a race or a play perhaps).

We hope you'll take the time to do the following exercise to help you determine what goals you want to work toward.

Exercise 1: Setting Goals and Establishing a Mission

Time required: 15 to 30 minutes total (three sessions)

Get as relaxed as you can. If you've had experience with meditation, autogenic training, self-hypnosis, or relaxation training, use it to get deeply relaxed. If not, sit in a comfortable chair, take a few deep, satisfying breaths, imagine a time in your life when you were very relaxed, and be as comfortable as possible.

Then allow your mind to consider what you most want to change in your life. Don't try to pin anything down right away. Just let yourself consider the possibilities. After a few minutes, you'll probably zero in on one or two things. If you don't zero in, that's fine. Just consider the possibilities that go through your mind and continue this for as long as you like.

When you have one or two items, allow them to get as specific as you can. As much as possible, imagine yourself achieving this ultimate goal.

When you are ready, allow yourself to consider your purpose in realizing this goal. A sentence, a word or two, or perhaps a picture will probably come to mind as your mission.

Finally, allow yourself to imagine what steps will lead you to achieve the ultimate goal. Don't try to be comprehensive or completely accurate. Just take what comes up as short-range stepping-stones toward your goal.

When you want, open your eyes and write down your ultimate goal, your mission, and your short-range goals. Then put your paper away in a safe place and leave it there for a day or two. Meanwhile, you may want to continue reading this book and get started on the relaxation techniques in chapter 6. When you come back to your list of goals, review what you've written and see if you want to change anything. It's common to want to make changes. The ultimate goal may be too ambitious or not ambitious enough. You may want to word your mission in stronger terms. And there may be one or more means (short-term goals) you want to add. Picture yourself achieving the goals and doing the necessary work. Make the changes you want and again put your paper away. Come back to it again in two or three days and repeat the process. At the end of this third session, you should have a pretty good idea of what you want, why you want it, and what you're going to have to do to get there.

* *

Keep in mind that what you have written can be changed later on if necessary. If it turns out that you've been too ambitious, you can always scale things down. If you've underestimated your abilities, you can always escalate. Changes should not be a matter of whim or impulse — if you make them too easily, every day or week, you'll never have a long-range program — but they can be made if circumstances dictate.

Some people have trouble deciding what goals to shoot for. Either they aren't clear about what they want to begin with or doing the above exercise confuses them: no goals seem worthy or possible, or there are too many to choose from. If you have problems like this, we suggest you let go of goal setting for now, continue reading, and do the relaxation exercises. Usually something will present itself before too long. If you have difficulty choosing between several goals, go by whim or flip a coin. It really doesn't make much difference. You can always go after another one later.

Once you are satisfied with your goals and mission, we suggest you rewrite them on a clean sheet of paper and keep that paper in a safe place or post it prominently (on your bedroom wall, or on the refrigerator, for instance). It will be useful to look at it as you move through your program.

Now that you have your goals in mind, it's time to consider this: How important is it for you to achieve them? Most people answer something like "very important," but that's too vague. There are many very important goals in everyone's life, but not all can be realized. It costs to get what you want. If nothing else, it takes time and energy that cannot at the same time be used for other things.

The following exercise will help you determine what you need to do to achieve your goals. It's important that you be as realistic as possible in doing it. Do not make the common error of assuming that once you begin your program you will suddenly be infused with extra energy or that your days will magically be lengthened to thirty-five hours. Most people who are realistic quickly discover that they need to take time from other activities and that substitution usually turns out to be one of the main costs of making the changes they desire.

Exercise 2: Determining if You Can Do What Is Necessary

Time required: 15 minutes total (one or more sessions)

As in the first exercise, allow yourself to relax. Then consider the time, effort, and energy it will require for you to meet your goals. The mental training will take only a few minutes a day, but it needs to be done every day to be most effective and needs to be done when you're relatively fresh and alert. Don't be seduced by the superficial association between relaxation and sleep. It's very hard to do useful work with your mind when you're falling asleep.

In most cases, there will be other things to be done — taking courses, getting consultation, doing physical training, and so on. Make sure you include realistic estimates of the time these activities will take.

Then consider where the time and energy are going to come from. Are you really willing to wake up or come home or get to the gym earlier? Are you really willing to stop going to the consultant, coach, or therapist that you feel hasn't been giving you what you want? Are you really willing to stop reading the newspaper or watching the news on TV every evening, to stop visiting your mother every Sunday, to give up talking to your friend Susie for twenty or thirty minutes every day, or to stop driving the kids around so much?

Allow these considerations to be with you for as long as needed. Don't pressure yourself to come up with quick answers. You may find you can't come up with a definite answer in one session; if so, take as many as you need over a week or two.

* *

By the end of this exercise, whether done in one or more sessions, you should arrive at one of three answers. One is that you desire the changes you want enough to take time and energy from other places; you know exactly what you need to do to get the time, and you're going to do it immediately. If that is the case, you are ready to go on to the next chapter.

Another possibility is that the goals are important but you're not sure exactly where to get the time to pursue them. If that's your situation, it's important to take as much time as necessary getting things straightened out *before* you start a program. Do not start doing the exercises in the rest of this book until you have time and energy set aside for them. You might want to go over every single thing in your life that is not absolutely necessary to see what can be cut down or cut out.

The last possible response is that although you'd like to achieve the goals, you simply aren't willing to cut down on other things to gain the necessary time and energy. If that's the case, you have only three options: put the original goals on hold for now, perhaps pursuing them at a later time; go after other goals that require less effort; or try a program now in a haphazard fashion.

We urge you *not* to take the third option. Pursuing a self-change effort in a halfhearted way is most likely to result in failure. That will make you feel bad about yourself, hardly what you need, and will also make it harder to return to the same program at another time because the smell of failure will pervade it. Far better to do nothing or to pursue other goals than to undertake a program in anything less than a wholehearted way. It is not necessarily a cop-out to determine that now is not the best time to take on a big effort at change. Perhaps sometime in the future will be better for you.

Now that you know your ultimate goals, the means to them, and where the time and energy will come from, it's time to start going after them.

Imagination grows by exercise.
      — Somerset Maugham

CHAPTER 5

THE MECHANICS OF
MENTAL TRAINING

This chapter is crucial to your use of mental training. It gives the nuts and bolts you'll need — how to proceed from here, guidelines to follow in your program, some things you should know about mental imagery, and how best to make and use tape recordings.

How to Proceed

As indicated earlier, we devote a chapter to each of the basic methods of mental training. Each chapter also contains at least one detailed example of someone using that method to achieve certain results. You are going to devise your own program, your own way of using the methods we offer. Don't let that statement worry you; we provide plenty of guidelines along the way. Using our examples and suggestions, you'll come up with what works best for you, and you'll be on your way.

The first thing to do is read the rest of this chapter.

Then go back to the last chapter and set your goals if you haven't already done so. If you're not ready to do that, then continue reading and perhaps our examples will help you decide what you want to do. After you've set your goals, you'll be ready to start the relaxation exercises. During the days or weeks you're practicing relaxation, you should read the rest of the book. As you read, look for cases and techniques that seem relevant to your situation. Underline or otherwise mark passages, exercises, examples and pages of interest, because you'll want to return to them later.

After you have had some experience with your relaxation tape, return to the book and look at an example or two that is most similar to your situation. You might also want to glance through the rest of the book, noting passages that you marked the first time through. Then make a list, under the goal you've written down, of the exercises you want to use to achieve it.

At this point, if you're like a lot of people we've worked with, you may experience some anxiety as questions such as these arise: "How do I know which methods are best?" "In what order should I use them?" Not to worry. The best methods are the ones that work for you, meaning the ones that you like and are willing to use. As for the order in which to use them, we give suggestions throughout the book. For example, we note that in working with goal imagery and process imagery, it's often helpful to start with an image of having achieved your ultimate goal and to keep using that one while working with process images. The suggestions in the rest of this chapter and the rest of the book will help you design a program that is right and effective for you.

As you devise your own program and carry it out, try to keep in mind that there are no secrets and no magic methods. Therapists, coaches, and others who teach mental training have only their own experiences and the results of somewhat inconclusive research to go on. The research is inconclusive in that it doesn't clearly say what methods work best for different people. And therapists, consultants, coaches, and others have their own biases; often they'll choose to use favorite methods that aren't necessarily appropriate for a particular client. There is some trial and error in all human endeavors, so there's no reason for concern if everything you try doesn't work out as you want. Learn from such experiences and try something else.

Guidelines for Your Mental-Training Program

• *Take it seriously.* Mental training requires some work, but whether it's a lot of work or not depends on what you're comparing it to. Certainly it is less work than what is usually required in psychotherapy and most kinds of athletic and artistic training. The techniques we offer have proved effective countless times, and almost all the people who use them believe the work is well worth it.

One of the main mistakes people make when undertaking a self-help program is to be casual about it. Instead of doing the exercises in the prescribed manner, they skip essential steps; instead of being systematic, they are cavalier. And then they get angry with the developers of the program when it doesn't bring about desired changes.

Let's be as clear as we can about this point: Making changes requires thoughtful and systematic effort, and there is simply no way around this. Both of us have written self-help books and have often encountered the following problem. People call up to make an appointment, saying they tried what was in our books but failed to make the changes they wanted. It usually turns out that although they read our material, they didn't apply it the way we suggested in the books.

One man said angrily that he still ejaculated prematurely during sexual intercourse even though he religiously applied our methods. What he didn't say until later, during his first appointment, was that his religious application lasted only a week. Neither of us had ever said that premature ejaculation can be overcome in a week or that any other important changes can occur in such a short period. Other people simply don't apply the material at all in a reasonable fashion. They do exercises "only when I think about it," or they use shortened (and less effective) versions of what is suggested.

We don't want to confuse you with that last sentence. You need to arrange your mental-training program so it best suits your situation and preferences. We often suggest that you make modifications to suit yourself. That is perfectly acceptable. What is not acceptable, on the other hand, is deciding that a one-line variation of a two-page script is all you'll need.

If the improvements you want to make are important to you, you're going to have to give yourself the time and energy to devote to them. Don't shortchange yourself. These methods work. Give yourself the best shot at making them work for you.

• *Keep written notes.* Many people find it helpful to keep written lists and notes when going through a self-help program. They keep track of each method they use, recording dates, results, and anything else that seems relevant. From time to time they review their notes and learn something in the process. This type of note-taking and occasional review is an excellent way to learn from both successes and failures and to keep moving in the desired direction.

While we heartily recommend the keeping of notes, we recognize that some people don't like to write notes and won't do it. These people can still make effective use of mental training, of course, but they will be better off if they do in their minds what others do on paper — keep track of what methods they use and what the results are. One way or another, it helps to remember what you've done and what works best for you.

• *Practice daily.* You should do some mental training every single day until you achieve your goals. That's the ideal but it's also realistic. You'll only need to devote a few minutes a day to your imagery, perhaps fifteen to twenty-five minutes at the start and five to fifteen minutes later on. That's less than what most meditation requires. It's really okay if you miss a day here and there, but don't overdo the missing of days. It's almost impossible to do too much mental training. *The more often you do it, the sooner you'll get what you want.* It's not unusual for athletes to do mental training ten, twenty, or even more times a day (though, to be sure, each time is short). We're not suggesting you should do it this often; we're merely repeating that there's no danger in doing lots of mental training.

Most of the people we've worked with have found it easiest to keep to a regular schedule — that is, to do their training at the same time(s) every day. Having regularly scheduled times ensures that the minimum will get done. If you want to do more, that's just frosting.

• *Practice, don't analyze.* It is important to understand that mental training is for doing, not analyzing. Some people, particularly those with experience in psychoanalytically oriented psychotherapies, make the mistake of looking for insights and understandings in their mental training. While it is true that sometimes a useful insight results from the training or something comes up that you want to mull over later, mental training as we use it is not intended for analysis or understanding. The results come from regular practice with images. In other words, the purpose of mental training is to train the mind in certain ways and not to look for understanding about why you are as you are. Why you so far have never won a large contract or had a good relationship may be an interesting question to think over with a consultant or on your own, but that is not what you should be doing in your mental training. Rather, you should be imagining yourself doing the things that will win you that contract or get you a better relationship.

• *Always start with the easy and gradually work up to the more difficult.* One of the most helpful principles in mental training is this: Always start with what you can comfortably handle and gradually work your way up to images that are more difficult. This is simply another way of saying take things gradually, in steps you can manage. Let's say you want to become more assertive with your spouse (or boss or friend). When you think of the things you'd like to be able to say to him or her, you'll see that they fall into an order going from easy (things you could say now if you psyched yourself up a bit) to very difficult (things you couldn't possibly say now). Start your imagery work with the easy things, going over them again and again until you are comfortable with them and actually able to say them. As this happens, include some of the more difficult statements in your imagery. As you become able to say these things, move up the list again in your imagery work.

Sometimes it's not as clear as this, but imagery has built-in safeguards. You may think, for instance, that it would be relatively easy to tell your husband that you're not pleased with his level of participation in housework. But when you're relaxed and try to imagine telling him that, you can't imagine the scene at all, or you can but only with great tension and difficulty. So you learn that this item is not as easy as you thought. No reason to get upset or to analyze it. Just move it up on your list and get on with things that really are easier, perhaps telling him to pick his socks up off the floor. As you develop more confidence and experience, it will become easier to imagine telling him about the housework.

The Meaning and Use of Imagery

Because mental training involves a lot of work with imagery, it is crucial that you understand exactly what images are and how to best use them.

An image is nothing but the way you represent objects and experiences in your mind. Although most people tend to think of images as primarily visual — "picture (or see) yourself on the beach" — the fact is that different people have different ways of imagining. Some people — often those who are architects, artists, or engineers — tend to be especially good at seeing images. Some people — many musicians, for instance — tend to hear things. When you ask them to recall being on the beach, they will probably hear beach sounds — waves breaking, music playing, people laughing. Although Arnold Schwarzenegger and Jack Nicklaus have highly developed visual modalities, the kinesthetic sense is dominant in many other athletes; that is, they tend to imagine feeling themselves moving, running, jumping, and so on. When they are asked to imagine being on the beach, their first images may have to do with the feel of running on the sand, the feel of themselves swimming, and so on. Very few people have highly developed senses of taste or smell, but perhaps you are one of those who do.

One very important point about all of this needs emphasis: There is no right way or best way of imaging. Your dominant mode of imaging, whatever it is, is right for you and will allow you to use mental training for your benefit.

Your images need to be as vivid (alive, rich, real) as

possible. One way of meeting this goal is to practice regularly. Another way is to bring in other senses after your dominant mode has come into play.

Always go with your dominant mode first. When we say imagine, don't take that as a synonym for "see." When you instruct yourself to imagine such and such, imagine it any way you can. If your primary mode is kinesthetic, then feel whatever the image or scene is. Get as deeply into the feel of it as possible; feel it on your skin, in your muscles and joints. And then try to bring one or more of the other senses into it. For instance, in our example of lying on the beach, if at first you feel yourself in the sand and the warming rays of the sun on your body, that's fine. But then attempt to hear the breaking waves (or the seagulls or whatever), to smell and taste the salt air or the cooking hot dogs, and to see the water, the sand, or whatever else reminds you of being on the beach. The more specific the images and the more senses involved, the more you'll really be there and the more you'll benefit.

Some people get deeply involved in an image even though they're using only one (or perhaps two) sensory modes. A good example is Marcel Proust's remembrance of things past, in the book of that name, after tasting a madeleine. His experience would be called age regression by hypnotists and shows what can be done sometimes with just one sense. If you are satisfied with just one or two modes, then stick with them.

Merged and Separated Imagery

An essential distinction in imagery concerns your perspective: whether you are watching yourself from outside your own body or from within it. Let's use our familiar lying-on-the-beach scene for illustration. In the first type of imagery, which we call *separated*, you are a spectator —

as if you were watching yourself on a movie screen in front of you. You are outside your body, watching yourself lying on the beach. You can see the back of your head and your face, things that in reality you can't see without visual aids. You also can see what's going on behind your body. In the second kind of imagery, which we call *merged,* you experience lying on the beach from within your own body. You can't see what's going on behind you, you can't see the back of your head, you can't see your face. This, of course, is like your everyday perspective as you look out at the world through your own eyes.

This distinction is important because people react differently to these two perspectives. For most people, merged imaging is more intense and therefore harder to do. Let's say you feel uneasy about asking a friend for a loan. It may be much easier to imagine the scene as if on a movie screen, watching yourself asking for the loan, than to imagine being in your own body and asking for it. In reality, of course, that's where you're going to be. This suggests the strategy to follow in your imagery work. First imagine yourself separated asking for the loan. Only after you're comfortable with that should you imagine yourself merged asking for the loan. When that feels good, you're ready to ask.

The distinction between merged and separated imagery has another important aspect. Often we are afraid of things when we don't imagine any distance between us and them. Phobics, for instance, tend to view their feared object or event from a totally merged perspective; there's no separation at all in their minds. All they see is this horrible thing coming at them or engulfing them. The first step in relief is to practice viewing the situation as if from a distance (separated). That is, instead of seeing a huge dog with bared teeth rushing toward them and tearing them apart, they should make a movie on a small screen and watch themselves watching a dog approaching. This is not a complete phobia cure, but it will help. It will also help if they imagine the dog as smaller, less well-defined, and without coloring (a subject we say more about shortly).

You should keep this distinction in mind as we proceed. When you imagine something difficult, first do so separated. Only after you've mastered this should you merge into the image, stepping into your body and seeing the scene from that vantage. If you are fearful about anything, check to see how you're seeing it. If you are merged, step out of the picture and watch it from a distance.

The Structure of Imagery

All of the mind's productions have both content and structure. Content (what the picture is about or what the voice is saying) is what most people focus on, as we do in most of this book, but there also is immense value in attending to and altering the structure of images.

What do we mean by dealing with the structure or attributes of imagery? Here's an illustration: We recently saw a client who had become obsessed with a woman despite the sound arguments of the more rational side of him. For several weeks he did almost nothing but think of her; he didn't pick up his mail during this time or go to work. He felt "out of control and trapped." In answer to our questions about the structure of his image, he said the woman was about six inches in front of him, larger than life, brightly colored, and very clear. We asked him to shrink her size, move her far away, drain the color, and make the picture fuzzy. As he did so, his demeanor changed and he said he felt much better. He used this process of altering the structure of his image whenever he thought of her for the next few days and the results were dramatic. He picked up his mail and returned to work, and in a few days he called the woman to tell her that their relationship wasn't going to work out.

It is important to realize that we did not talk with our client at length about what he should do about this relationship or about his job or mail. In other words, we pretty much left the content alone. All we did was help him change the attributes of his imagery so he could feel in charge rather than out of control. Once he had the tools to do that on his own, he made the right decisions for himself. The work we did with him took only a few minutes.

Here are some useful questions to ask about the structure and attributes of each of your images: Is it from a merged or separated perspective? Where in your field of vision is the image (in the center, off to the right, off to the left)? How near is it (inches away, a foot or two away, two to ten feet away, or even farther)? Is the image a still picture like a slide or photograph, or is there motion? Is it in color or black-and-white? Regardless of that answer, is it bright or dim? What about clarity — is it clearly defined or fuzzy? What about size — is the image life-size, larger than life, or smaller? If your image consists mainly of sound — that is, if you imagine hearing words or noises — is it loud or soft and what is the tempo and pitch?

The reason for all these questions has to do with intensity of feeling. The attributes of your image, the kinds of things we just asked about, determine how strongly you will feel about it. The stronger the feelings, the more activating power they have. You can easily change the intensity of your images and feelings by changing their attributes. You'll have to experiment to see what works best for you, but here are some ideas:

Merged imaging, closeness, larger size, and louder sounds usually increase intensity. If you want more intensity, merge into the image, move what you're looking at closer, and make everything larger and the sounds louder. You might also want to add color if the original image is black-and-white and make the colors brighter if they are already there. Fuzziness works against intensity, so make the picture as sharp and clear as you can. If there's no sound, you might want to add a mental sound track consisting of music you find powerful or inspirational. Movies tend to have more impact than a still picture, so add movement if you have only a still.

We do not want to give you the impression that a more intense image is always better. Sometimes you want less intensity — as was certainly the case with the obsessed man we just discussed — and you should change the structure of your imagery accordingly. Feeling intimidated, for instance, almost invariably involves an image of the other person being very close, very large, and in bright color, or else a very loud voice. If you push the image away, make it smaller, and take the color out of it (or lower the volume of the voice), the feeling of intimidation immediately subsides or disappears. You might want to do an experiment with this right now. Just recall someone or something that intimidated you and check how you're seeing the person or situation. Then make changes as we suggested and see how your feelings change.

This kind of internal reorganization is also extremely effective for people who are victims of strong inner voices telling them how bad they are or that they shouldn't be doing this or that. Adding a soundtrack of silly or inappropriate music such as "Old MacDonald Had a Farm" or calliope music can work wonders, as can changing the pitch and tempo of the voice. If you tell yourself you'll never amount to anything, do it very quickly in a high, squeaky voice and observe the results. You can also quickly change your mood by altering the tempo of your internal voices. Can you recall a time when you were working yourself into a frantic state by rapidly saying to yourself, "You're going to be late, you're going to be late," or "You've got to get it done, you've got to get it done"? Next time that happens, just slow down the tempo of the voice to a snail's pace and observe how your feelings change.

We hope you'll experiment with changing the attributes of your images as we periodically suggest in later chapters. It's especially important to try this when you want to increase or decrease the intensity of feeling you are deriving from your images.

Here are some other ideas for making the most effective use of images and verbal suggestions. Since there are a number, we'll remind you of them later and illustrate them in our examples.

• Make your images and suggestions as specific as possible. As you'll notice in our examples, we ask people to imagine themselves feeling confident in a particular situation or to imagine themselves saying such and such to a particular person or in a particular situation. It's fine to tell yourself that you're becoming more assertive and confident. It's even better to say that you're becoming more assertive in telling your spouse how you feel about the way he or she didn't follow through on a promise to cut the lawn and that you're feeling more confident as you do so.

• If your images aren't as clear as you'd like at first, don't worry. Keep practicing. Specificity, clarity, and involvement of other senses come with time and practice. If they still aren't as vivid as you want, it will probably help to practice imagining all sorts of things for a few days. For instance, look at an apple, then close your eyes and imagine the apple. Look at a car or a chair or a pen, then close your eyes and imagine it. Keep practicing like this for a while and your images will get clearer.

• Maintain control over your imagery. Many people have a tendency to drift off into their usual negative self-suggestion when practicing images. The tendency to do this is understandable — after all, they've had lots of practice with negative fantasies — but it's still destructive. This is one reason that we strongly encourage the use of tape recordings. The tapes supply a structure that makes deviation more difficult than when doing imagery work without tapes.

If you find yourself getting caught up in negative images — for example, imagining that you'll be speechless during your presentation or that the audience will react with boos and hisses — there's no need to get upset and no need to fight these images. Getting into a struggle with them only increases their power. The thing to do is simple: just refocus your attention on the positive imagery. If you keep doing this, you'll find that it becomes easier to do and that the negative fantasies either don't appear as often or don't have as much power. One day you'll surprise yourself; after a session you'll realize that you did exactly what was suggested on your tape and that the whole experience was positive, affirming, and very useful.

• Word suggestions and images positively rather than negatively. For instance, tell yourself how much comfort you'll feel rather than how much pain you won't; imagine yourself feeling comfortable, even if your goal is to be free of pain.

• Give yourself something to do, or, put differently, don't leave a vacuum. If you tell yourself you won't smoke or won't get angry, you're not giving yourself anything to do except sit there without smoking or stand there without being angry. It's very hard to imagine yourself *not* doing something. Better to suggest that you'll reach for a piece of candy or chewing gum (instead of a cigarette), or that you'll take a few deep breaths and feel surprisingly calm and uninvolved in your mother's comments (the thing that usually gets you angry). Action works best, so imagine yourself doing something that reflects the feeling or state you're seeking. Reaching for chewing gum is doing something, but the example of feeling calm about your mother's statement needs help. What would you do if you truly felt calm about it — continue talking with her, change the subject, kiss her? Whatever it is, use it.

• Use lots of repetition. Give suggestions a number of times, as per our examples, changing the wording slightly to add variety. You'll know you're being overrepetitive when it gets boring to listen to.

• Keep suggestions and images simple and concise. Don't try to pack too much into one suggestion, one image, or one session. Better to err on the side of too little than too much.

• Recall past successes to set the right emotional tone for your mental-training session and use them in post-hypnotic suggestions. (This is explained in chapter 7.)

• Treat yourself well in your training. Compliment and verbally reward yourself as much as possible. We cover this issue in detail in chapter 10.

The Value of Tape Recordings

Mental training works best with tapes, at least in the beginning. We will provide scripts for you to record and listen to, which will help guide your training in the initial stages. Without a tape you have to give a suggestion (for example, to imagine a certain scene) as well as carry it out. The giving of suggestions can be confusing at the beginning, can involve more of your rational processes than is helpful, and also can make it harder to relax. It is much easier just to listen to the directions and carry them out. The content of the tapes also provides structure to your sessions, making it easier to do what needs to be done and more difficult to wander off.

Although we devote space in this chapter and others to

the making of tapes, we realize that some readers won't want to make them. You may find it bothersome or feel that you're just not recording them correctly. There are two alternatives if you're in this group. One is to order the prerecorded exercise tape we've prepared (follow the instructions on the last page of this book). This tape offers a number of enhancements over homemade products by incorporating the latest in psychological and audio technologies. It is designed to be used in your own mental-training program and will guide you through the important exercises.

The other alternative is not to use tapes at all. If you choose this one, you'll need to read each exercise carefully several times, getting clear in your mind exactly what you're going to do while in trance. Then you will need to follow those steps in order. Although we do not recommend this way because it places a greater burden on you, we know people who've done it successfully. For reasons of clarity, we continue under the assumption that you will be making your own tapes.

What you need to make tapes is a cassette system that both records and plays back. If you don't already have such a recorder, you should consider borrowing or buying one. You don't need the best but you probably also don't want the cheapest because its quality, or lack of it, may interfere with your work. Decent cassette recorders can be bought for under fifty dollars. You'll need two or three blank cassette tapes with thirty minutes of recording time per side. While you don't need the kind of high-quality tape used to record a piano concerto, neither should you settle for the ten-for-a-dollar bargains. Their fidelity is often so bad as to interfere with listening.

In the next chapter, we give instructions for making your first tape. Unless you are already skilled at relaxation training, meditation, or self-hypnosis, do not go on to the other methods in this book without first making that relaxation tape and using it for a few days or in some other way getting some practice with relaxation.

Some people have trouble with their own tapes because they are self-conscious about their voices. "My God, do I sound like that?" is a fairly common reaction. Yes, you do sound like that, and it's fine. This self-consciousness typically disappears after a few minutes of listening. If it doesn't, or if you can't even think about listening to a recording of your own voice, you may want to order the tapes we've prepared.

Under no circumstances should you listen to a relaxation tape or other mental-training tape while driving a car or operating machinery. To do so is very dangerous. The purpose of the tapes is to take you inward, but when operating machinery or driving you need to have all your attention available to deal with other people and other machines.

Although tapes are what you will be using in most of your work, many people find that the process works best if they have someone else guide them the first time or two. So you may want to have someone experienced in mental training — a therapist, coach, or friend — guide you through your first few sessions. If you don't know anyone with these skills, you can enlist an untrained friend or spouse to read one of the relaxation exercises in chapter 6 to you. After one or two repetitions, you can make your own tape of the same procedure.

The purpose of the tapes is simply to help you master a skill like relaxation or a certain kind of imagery. After you have a week or so of practice with a particular image, you probably won't need the tape anymore. So use the image without the tape and make another tape for the next image you want to employ.

General Guidelines for Making and Using Mental-Training Tapes

• The physical setting where you make your tapes need not be the same as the one where you listen to them, but they should both be as quiet as possible and free of interruptions. Some people choose an appropriate place for listening but make the tapes in any old place, no matter how noisy and full of distractions. This is an error because anything that can be heard during the recording session will be heard when you're listening to the tape. And if you're anxious about being interrupted or about noises when recording, that feeling will come through on the tape.

• Before making any tapes, familiarize yourself with the workings of your recorder. Be sure you know what buttons to press to make it record, to make it play back, and to stop it. When you go to record a script, be sure the right button is on. It's as easy to record without having the record button on as it is to take pictures without having film in your camera. Even after years of making tapes, we still sometimes forget to turn the record button on before recording.

• After turning on your machine and the record button, allow fifteen to twenty seconds to go by before beginning to speak. That will give you a little time during listening to get settled before you hear the first words.

• Hold the microphone at a constant distance from your mouth while recording and speak slowly, in normal conversational voice. There's no need to try to sound like Vincent Price or to imitate a stage hypnotist you may have heard. Just be yourself, remembering that your self has feeling and intention. When you try to help someone relax, you probably speak in a soothing voice. So speak soothingly when you make a relaxation tape and put some oomph into your voice when you talk about power and confidence. In other words, be natural and don't be afraid to ham it up and have a good time.

• When making recordings, don't expect the impossible. It's true that the ideal would be a recording with no slurred words, no wrong words, and no distracting noises such as coughs and those that result from turning the machine off and on. If you listen to the tapes we offer for sale, you'll find they come close to this ideal. But these tapes are made in highly contrived conditions with a great deal of preparation and very sophisticated equipment (which, among other things, eliminates the sound of turning the recorder off and on). The tapes we make in our offices for our clients aren't half as polished but they work quite well.

If you stumble over a word or phrase, don't worry about it; just continue recording and say it correctly. If you cough or sneeze, just keep on reading. If you lose your place and leave a longer gap than what you wanted, that's fine; just keep on going. If you need to stop for whatever reason, that's also fine. Just turn off the recorder, or use the pause button if it has one, and then resume (remembering to turn the pause button off or the record button on) when you're ready.

Keep in mind that with experience you'll feel more comfortable and get better at making recordings. But we guarantee you that even years of experience does not make for perfection. We're sure the tapes you make will be just fine.

• The best environment for listening to tapes is one in which you are free from distractions and feel comfortable, safe, and ready for the experience. Adjust the lighting to what you like and make sure you won't be surprised by phones, co-workers, or other interruptions. People often find that a comfortable high-backed chair, especially if it reclines, is best. Lying in bed works for some people but not for others because it tempts them into sleep. You need a different arrangement if you find that you're falling asleep when listening to the tapes. We strongly recommend listening through earphones. This intensifies the power of the recording, making it, as one person said, "your whole world." The earphones need not be expensive. The kind provided with Sony's Walkman and similar cassette players is fine.

After you've had more experience, you'll probably find that you can listen to tapes or practice without them in almost any setting: while waiting for a phone call, on a bus or train or plane, or during a ten-minute break at work. But in the early phases, it's best to have as quiet a setting as possible.

• To repeat something we said earlier: Never, ever, listen to a relaxation tape or other mental-training tape while driving a car or operating machinery.

Guidelines for Using Mental-Training Scripts

The scripts are set up in a way that makes them easy to understand and follow. The words you are to read are in boldface type. Pauses — times during which you say nothing but keep the recorder running — are indicated by a series of dots (. . . .). We would like to be able to define in seconds how long pauses should be, but there is no way. A pause needs to be long enough for you to carry out the suggestion before it (for example, "take a deep, satisfying breath") but not so long as to make you fidget. Pauses can last anywhere from three to thirty seconds. You'll have to do what we do: experiment. Your mind will accommodate itself to the pauses you give it, but if you find yourself rushing to carry out the suggestions, that means you should use longer pauses on your next tape. On the other hand, if you start to get restless, make the pauses shorter next time.

There's something else you'll have to experiment with. Some people don't like much silence on a tape. When carrying out a suggestion such as to take a deep breath, they like words of encouragement during the activity (for instance, "that's right, in and out, a nice deep breath"). Others prefer silence when they're carrying out a suggestion. Do whatever is right for you.

Here and there within the scripts, we have added specific instructions or asked you to insert your own wording. (These passages, which are italicized and enclosed in brackets, are not to be recorded verbatim.) If you own this book, you can use the page margins to write changes to the script and any additional notes you want to make. Here are some general guidelines for using the scripts:

• Before recording a script, read it aloud several times to get comfortable with it. As you read through a script the first time, you will come across our italicized remarks about specific material you should insert. Take some time to decide exactly what that material is and how you want to word it. Your statements should be included the last time you read the script through *before* recording it.

• Don't take our estimates for the duration of a script too seriously. They are only approximations. The duration of a tape depends on how fast you talk and how long your pauses are.

• Feel free to alter the scripts to suit your needs. You should definitely replace any words and phrases that offend or startle you. You should definitely include more repetition if that seems warranted. The scripts need to be easy to hear, easy for you to accept, and easy to follow. It is crucial that nothing in them jars or upsets you. Anything that helps achieve these ends should be tried, even if that means altering the script.

You now have the essential information for setting goals, recording tapes, and using mental training. Now, on to the specifics.

A quiet mind cureth all.
    — Robert Burton

CHAPTER 6

GETTING RELAXED

In this chapter we describe and help you attain the relaxation skills useful in the practice of mental training. But there are many routes to relaxation and perhaps you already know one or more. If you have experiece with yoga, meditation, biofeedback, autogenic training, or the relaxation exercises involved in natural childbirth, you may not need what we present here and can skip to the next chapter.

Or perhaps you have some other way of relaxing that works well for you. A number of people we've worked with over the years have told us about relaxation methods they developed on their own. One harried executive, for instance, says all he has to do to get deeply relaxed is settle back in a chair, close his eyes, and imagine being in his first-class seat on a long airplane flight, where no one can reach him and with no work to do, just looking out of the window at the sky. A few moments of this and he feels very much at peace. In our work with him, we asked him to go through this procedure, signaling when he was ready for our suggestions. Another busy executive says that all she has to do is close her eyes and hear her mother singing a lullaby to her, as was the case when she was a child.

A number of people have told us they get deeply relaxed listening to the music of Steven Halpern, Kitaro, George Winston, Georgia Kelly, or Daniel Kobialka. Classical pieces such as Pachelbel's Kanon and various compositions of Bach and Chopin have also been used to good effect. If you find that a certain piece works for you, feel free to use it alone or in conjunction with taped suggestions. These might be similar to ones we use. With the music playing, we say things like: "Just ride the music, allowing it to take you deeper and deeper to a beautiful, wonderful, restful place of increasing comfort and calm . . . . more and more at peace."

If you have an effective method of your own, by all means use it.

Numerous studies have shown that positive imagery and suggestions work best when you are relaxed. The altered state brought on by relaxation is subtly but considerably different from your everyday waking state and is the only prerequisite for using the powerful techniques of mental training. There is little point in using the material in the rest of this book until you have achieved some proficiency at relaxing yourself. (We should mention, however, that studies indicate that a small number of people have great difficulty getting relaxed or, paradoxically, get more tense when trying to relax. If you already know you're in this group, or find you are after trying some of the relaxation exercises that follow, there's no need to despair. You can still use mental training. See our discussion on page 123 about recalling past successes.)

Relaxation is a natural human capacity, one we are all born with, and while learning or relearning to relax as an adult takes a little practice, it's not very difficult. Almost anyone can learn to become more comfortable, calmer, more relaxed.

Notice that relaxation is not the same as recreation. Many people say "I relax with a good book," or "I find TV relaxing." They are confusing relaxation with recreation. While recreation is both positive and important, it is not the same as letting go of muscular tension in a systematic way, so that deeper and deeper levels of relaxation are attained.

Numerous well-controlled studies show that relaxation training is extremely effective in combating stress, diminishing anxiety, decreasing hypertension, and overcoming a wide range of bodily ills. Most people find that they experience a significant reduction in subjective anxiety when they deliberately "let go" of tense muscles. When a person enters into a state of deep muscle relaxation, pulse rate and blood pressure decrease, respiration becomes slower and more regular — all healthy, calming qualities. Some readers may find that regular practice with relaxation is all they need to accomplish their goals. Spending fifteen to thirty minutes a day relaxing can make a big difference, as many people who meditate have discovered. The main problem with relaxation techniques and meditation is that most people don't continue doing them for long. Because our methods are shorter than most of the others available, we have been successful in having people continue with them for months and even years.

The pioneer of relaxation training, Dr. Edmund Jacobson, developed a most elaborate method called *progressive relaxation*. His basic thesis was that it is impossible to be upset or uptight while fully relaxed, because relaxation and nervous tension are physiological opposites. Many therapists use Jacobson's progressive relaxation, but this method is much more detailed and time-consuming than necessary. Jacobson thought that it took two months of daily practice before someone could relax his or her whole body. Fortunately, most people will derive great benefit from shorter and less taxing methods. The level of relaxation required to derive full benefit from mental training is not especially profound. Basically, you just need be a little less tense, a little more relaxed, than you normally are. At the beginning, five-to-ten-minute sessions may be necessary, but within a week or so of daily practice, the time required can be cut down to a very few minutes.

Before we go any further, perhaps you would like to try a simple relaxation exercise. Sit down, or lie down, and get as comfortable as you can. Take in a deep breath, hold it for a moment, and exhale. Now make a fist, really hard, tighter and tighter, almost to the point of cramping. Notice the uncomfortable tension in your hand, fingers, and forearm. Hold that tension for about ten seconds. Then let all the tension go: relax your hand, open your fingers, let your hand rest limply on your lap, and notice the difference in your sensations. Now do the same with your other hand: make a very tight fist and study the tension and hold it for about ten seconds. Then relax your hand, let it rest comfortably on your lap or at your side, and observe the difference in your sensations. Now clench both fists really hard for about ten seconds, and then let go and study the difference between the tension sensations and the relaxation response.

Even this very brief preliminary tension-relaxation sequence will show you how unpleasant tension can be, and what a relief it is to let go of the tension. Some relaxation trainers recommend the alternate tensing and relaxing of every major muscle group, one by one. We used to employ this method but more recently we have achieved better results by omitting the tension and by dwelling only on the relaxation.

We have found that *cue (or key) words or phrases* are beneficial in relaxation and other mental-training work and we will ask you to come up with one or more in the scripts. A cue word or phrase is simply something that summarizes and represents to you a certain state or condition. Psychiatrist David Soskis of the University of Pennsylvania gives a nice example of what such a phrase can do. An outstanding runner came to him for help with "the wall," a sense of overwhelming fatigue and physical resistance that overtook him about three-quarters of the way through a race. He had gotten so tense anticipating the wall that he was running poorly even at the start of races.

Dr. Soskis worked with him to find a key phrase associated with a relaxing scene he liked. The runner came up with *strong and steady* — how he felt when imaging the relaxing scene and the opposite of how he felt when he hit the wall. The plan was to practice using this phrase repeatedly while relaxed, and then to repeat the words during races as he neared the place where he usually hit the wall. It worked very well. The runner felt much stronger and steadier in his running — because that's what he'd been telling himself he would feel — and he improved his time. Soon he found that using the key phrase *strong and steady* was automatic and he could devote his attention to positioning himself for the finish.

The runner's cue words, *strong and steady,* are also chosen by a large number of people we've worked with, along with variations such as *calm and strong, calm and cool,* and *resolute and relaxed.* Some people have just one word, often said with a special inflection, such as *serene, comfy, relaxed,* and *easy.* Like the runner, with steady practice they soon find themselves using these words automatically and virtually all report benefits from having these words replace the ones they used to say to themselves.

You choose your cue word or phrase simply by allowing your mind to come up with it when you're in the state you want later to replicate. When you're feeling very relaxed, for example, you just ask yourself, "What word or phrase represents this feeling to me?" As with almost everything else in mental training, it's important that the cue you come up with is your own. Even if others might not understand how *lettuce* or *Rocky* can signify comfort or competence, if they signify that to you, then that's what you should use.

There are several different types of relaxation-training programs. We will now provide typical training scripts containing some of the most effective procedures. We suggest you read over all the methods and then try several that appeal to you; as you try them, you'll see which work best. Some people prefer to stay with just one method they can count on, while others enjoy alternating among several.

When you decide which ones you want to try, either read the suggestions into a tape recorder or have someone read them to you as you follow what they say. There is nothing sacrosanct in how you relax. You can use one or more methods exactly as we present them or you can take elements of different methods to put together one that better suits you. If there's a phrase or sentence in one exercise that appeals to you, feel free to use it with another relaxation technique. If a word, phrase, or procedure bothers you, substitute something else. For instance, we sometimes use the word *heavy* to describe how some people feel when relaxed. But if this word offends you or doesn't work for you, replace it with *limp, loose, a floating sensation,* or anything else that does work.

The only criterion is that at the end of a relaxation session you truly do feel more relaxed. Common reactions are: "a wonderful and pleasant experience," "a nice warm feeling," "really comfortable," "like a dream," "very relaxed," "like floating on a cloud," and "very calm, very nice." If you feel anything like this, you've got it. Don't assume you're supposed to be a zonked-out zombie — just a little calmer, a little more comfortable, a little more relaxed.

If you don't feel more relaxed after an exercise, something is wrong and you need to determine what. Perhaps you're being distracted by noise or lack of privacy, perhaps you're worried about time because you have to leave for an appointment, perhaps you've chosen an exercise that simply isn't for you. Try a different one and make sure you have privacy and as much time as you need. You may also want to experiment with the structure of your images (as discussed on pages 78–83). For example, if you're picturing yourself relaxing on a beach from a separated perspective, try merging into the image and see what that does. Saying your cue word in a different way — for instance, more soothingly or more slowly — may also help. Do whatever you need to do to feel more comfort.

After a week or so of listening to the tape at least once and preferably twice a day, you can start doing the exercise from memory, reserving the tape for times when you are highly stressed or feel in need of a refresher course. Please remember that before starting to use any of the relaxation exercises, it is important that you sit down, or lie down, and get really comfortable. Make sure that your head and neck are adequately supported. Uncross your legs. Let your arms rest on your lap or at your sides. It is generally advisable to close your eyes while practicing the relaxation, to remove external distractions. It is sometimes uncomfortable for people who wear contact lenses to keep their eyes closed for extended periods. If this applies to you, you may want to remove your lenses before practicing the relaxation sequences. Also, it is a good idea to loosen any tight clothing, and to take off your shoes if this will add to your overall comfort. Although we recommend having your eyes closed during the relaxation training, some people, for various reasons, prefer to keep their eyes open.

Do whatever feels best for you. One final point: if possible, try to find a room where the noise level is low, the illumination is somewhat dim, and where you will not be disturbed or interrupted for at least fifteen minutes.

Let us remind you of some of the guidelines regarding scripts that we gave in the last chapter. Before recording any script, read it aloud several times until you feel comfortable with it. The words you will record are in boldface type. A series of dots indicates pauses, times when you should keep the recorder running and either be silent or make comments to help you carry out the suggestion that precedes the dots. Within the script, enclosed in brackets, are some italicized "stage directions" to help you (these are not to be recorded) and some requests for information for you to insert in the script. When you are ready to record, turn the record button on, let the tape run fifteen to twenty seconds, and then begin reading at a slow, regular pace and with a neutral or soothing tone. Don't rush.

Two more things about the relaxation exercises. First, the wording in them is not always consistent with formal grammar. Don't get hung up by this. You can change the words if you want; we use the particular phraseology because we have found it to be helpful. Second, keep in mind that relaxation is basically doing nothing and allowing something to happen. Relaxation cannot be forced and there's no need to *try* to be relaxed. Just let it happen.

We start with breathing exercises because respiration is so very closely connected to fear, tension, and anxiety — and opposite reactions such as serenity, calmness, and self-confidence. By gaining control of your breathing when in a frightening situation, you will experience an immediate sense of control and a lesser degree of anxiety. In other words, if you experience discomfort in a stressful situation, you will gain a sense of comfort and self-control by deliberately breathing slowly and deeply. Similarly, for most people, taking a few deep, satisfying breaths is the quickest and most effective road to greater relaxation.

Script 1: Relaxation via Deep Breathing and Relaxing Imagery

Time required: 7 to 10 minutes

Take as much time as you need to get really settled and really comfortable. Find the best position for your body as you begin to let go of tension and enter ever deeper levels of comfort and relaxation. This is a time for your pleasure, for your comfort, for yourself. . . . .

When you feel settled and the beginnings of comfort, take several deep, satisfying breaths, but not just yet. For the breaths to be as relaxing as possible, it's important that they be deep and satisfying, but without any kind of effort or hassle. As much as possible, you want to breathe into your belly, so that inhalations cause your stomach to protrude a bit. When your lungs are full, hold the breath a moment or two, but not to the point of discomfort. When you feel like it, and only when you feel like it, exhale slowly and comfortably, allowing the air to carry away any tensions you have with it, disappearing into the air. A deep, satisfying exhalation. And then when you want, take another deep, satisfying breath, bringing in fresh, life-giving air, breathing out stale, tense air, carrying your tensions with it, leaving you feeling lighter, calmer, more relaxed.

Now, when you want, start taking the first of nine or ten really satisfying breaths. . . . .

[You need to leave enough time to take these breaths, but silence is neither necessary nor advisable. As you take the breaths, the words in the rest of this paragraph, or variations on them, should be used, with pauses between them, to encourage your deepening relaxation.]

With each exhalation, imagine tension leaving your body, going out with the air, leaving you feeling more comfortable, more

serene, really nice. . . . . That's right, more and more relaxed. . . . . Tension going out, relaxation coming in. . . . .
Relaxing deeper and deeper, feeling freer and more at ease. . . . .

And when you're done with nine or ten deep, satisfying
breaths, you can just breathe normally or, if you want, take a
few more deep, satisfying, and relaxing breaths. . . . .

To help you relax even further, just let yourself use your
mind, that powerful tool that is so helpful in relaxing and
making changes that you desire. As you sit there comfortably
relaxed, imagine a relaxing scene.

[Here you should use a scene that is relaxing to you. We use the example
of lying on a beach. If this works for you, use it; otherwise, use your
own scene and give suggestions, as we do, to encourage imaging it as
clearly as possible. If you do use the beach scene, include the name of
your beach.]

Recall lying on your blanket on a beautiful beach and as you
do, allow yourself to relax even further. Feel the warming rays
of the sun on your head, your back, your legs. . . . . Feel the
blanket under you, warm and comforting. . . . . Can you hear
the waves breaking, one after the other? . . . . Smell the cooking
hot dogs and the salty smell of the sea in the air. . . . . How
comforting and pleasant it is to be on the beach, with nothing
to do, nowhere to go, just relaxing, just being. . . . . And as you
imagine being on the beach, just being and relaxing, allow
yourself as much comfort and as much pleasure as you can,
letting go and letting be, just lying there. . . . . There's nothing
to do and nowhere to go, so you might as well enjoy and relax
and be, and that's very nice. Allow yourself to enjoy the pleasant moment as long as you want. . . . . And maybe you're realizing that it's not so bad to be fully relaxed and comfortable.

Now let your mind come up with a word or phrase that
represents this nice, safe, pleasant feeling.

[You can pick out your cue word or phrase ahead of time or when listening
to the tape. It might be "relaxed," "calm," "serene," "safe," or some
combination of these or other words. It doesn't make any difference as

long as the word or words are associated with the wonderful, relaxed feelings you're now having.]

Good, and now repeat [*use your actual cue word or phrase here*] **every time you exhale. Repeat it several times to yourself. . . . . With some practice, when you say** [*use your cue word here*] **to yourself, it will bring back the warm, relaxed, safe feelings you're now experiencing. Now do it one more time. Repeat** [*your cue word*] **several times, each time feeling the wonderful relaxing feelings that go with it. . . . . Very good.**

When you feel you're finished with the experience and want to come back to your everyday consciousness, just count backwards to yourself from five to one, feeling more alert, more awake with each number. When you get to one, your eyes will be open, you'll be awake, alert, and fully functioning. Five . . . . four, more alert . . . . three . . . . halfway there . . . . two, eyes starting to open . . . . and one, refreshed, awake, fully alert, and still relaxed. You may want to wiggle around a bit to re-orient yourself.

The goal to work toward with the first script is to be able to relax just by closing your eyes and repeating your cue word, by taking a few deep breaths, or by imagining your relaxing scene. This cannot be done in a day. It takes regular practice with the tape for a week or two or three, and regular practice with the short forms of relaxation (breaths, cue words, or relaxing images).

The next relaxation method sounds a bit strange. It was brought to our attention by Dr. Gerald C. Davison of the University of Southern California and Dr. Marvin R. Goldfried of the State University of New York at Stony Brook. They, in turn, give credit to Dr. Bernard Weitzman of the New School for Social Research. We have modified it to some extent in line with the experience of our own clients. Although it sounds funny and although it is not widely used, we have found it very effective for some people. If its strangeness or brevity appeal to you, give it a try. You should sit in a chair or sofa that is high enough to support your back and neck.

In this exercise, the pauses indicated by the series of dots at the end of each question should all be five seconds.

Script 2: Relaxation by Sensory Awareness

Time required: 5 minutes

Begin by getting as comfortable as you can. Please listen very closely to the specific questions that you will be asked. Each question can be answered by "yes" or "no." It is not necessary for you to say "yes" or "no" out loud. There is no right or wrong answer. What is important is only your own particular reaction to the question. Do not bother about the unusual nature of some of the questions. Let yourself react to each question. However you react is fine. Remember, allow your own reaction to be your answer to each question. . . . .

• Is it possible for you to allow your eyes to close? . . . .

• If your eyes are closed, is it possible for you to keep them closed throughout the remainder of these questions? . . . .

• Is it possible for you to be aware of the point at which the back of your head comes into maximum contact with the chair? . . . .

• Is it possible for you to imagine the space between your eyes? . . . .

• Is it possible for you to imagine the distance between your ears? . . . .

• Is it possible for you to become aware of your breathing? . . . .

• Is it possible for you to imagine that you are looking at something that is far away in the distance? . . . .

• Is it possible for you to notice a warm feeling somewhere in your body? . . . .

• Is it possible for you to be aware of where your arms are in contact with the chair? . . . .

• If your feet are resting on the floor, can you feel the floor beneath them? . . . .

• Is it possible for you to imagine the space within your mouth? . . . .

• Is it possible for you to be aware of one of your arms being more relaxed than the other? . . . .

• Is it possible for you to be aware of one of your legs being more relaxed than the other? . . . .

• Is it possible for you to notice a relaxed feeling somewhere inside your body? . . . .

• Is it possible for you to feel even the slightest breeze against your cheek? . . . .

• Is it possible for you to be aware of the position of your tongue within your mouth? . . . .

• Is it possible for your entire body to feel pleasantly heavy and calm? . . . .

• Is it possible for you to imagine once again that you are looking at something that is very far away? . . . .

• Is it possible for you to imagine in your mind's eye a beautiful flower suspended a few feet in front of you? . . . .

And now just allow yourself to be as relaxed and peaceful as you like and enjoy this feeling for as long as you desire. . . . . .

If your eyes are closed, can you allow them to open? . . . . And if they're not yet open you may open them now and feel wide awake and yet relaxed and comfortable.

The next method systematically goes through all the muscle groups of the body, relaxing each in turn. It takes longer than the others, but has worked very well for many people, especially those who do not respond to the shorter methods. The second part of this approach, relaxing by counting backwards from ten to one, is used in a number of hypnotic inductions and appeals to many people. If you desire, you can of course use that part with another relaxation exercise.

Script 3: Relaxation by Letting Go

Time required: 10 to 12 minutes

Sit down or lie down and get comfortable. Make sure that all parts of your body are supported so that there is no need to tense any muscles. Most people find that they relax more deeply with their eyes closed. Begin by taking in a very deep breath. Fill your lungs and hold your breath. . . . . And now exhale and then continue breathing normally, in and out. Try to sense a definite calming sensation beginning to develop. . . . . Now focus on the feelings in your forehead and scalp, and feel your forehead smoothing out as a wave of relaxation spreads comfortably throughout your head, face, neck, and throat. . . . . Let your lips part slightly as your jaws relax. . . . . And allow your tongue to rest comfortably in your mouth, as you observe the pleasant feelings of relaxation in your throat and neck area. . . . .

As you continue letting go, feel the relaxation proceeding down your right arm so that it feels pleasantly heavy. . . . . Now focus on your right hand and let go of whatever tensions might be there. . . . . Feel your right arm relaxing, getting pleasantly heavy, from your shoulders all the way down to your fingertips. . . . . You may feel a tingling sensation or even a feeling of floating at times, which are signs that tight muscles are loosening. While you continue letting go of the tension in your right arm and hand, turn your attention to your left arm, and allow the relaxation to proceed down your left arm and into your left hand. . . . . Just let go further and further. Now your head, jaws, and face are relaxed, your neck and throat are relaxed, your shoulders and arms are relaxed, all the way down to the tips of your fingers. . . . . Just let go further and further, becoming more and more relaxed. . . . .

Now turn your attention to your chest and stomach. As you inhale and exhale, there is a gentle, rhythmic, massaging action that loosens tight chest muscles and allows your abdomen and stomach area to relax..... Let go further and further..... Relax more and more..... Feel the relaxation in your hips and buttocks as you rest comfortably, becoming further and more deeply relaxed..... Continue letting go more and more..... Now sense the relaxation in your thighs .... and into the calves of both your left and right legs, becoming more and more relaxed..... Now let the relaxation down into both your feet, further and more deeply relaxed.....

Now, one by one, you'll think of each separate part to be relaxed. As you think of each part, allow yourself to feel the relaxation becoming even deeper, part by part .... hands .... forearms .... upper arms .... shoulders .... neck .... jaws .... mouth .... tongue .... eyes .... forehead .... chest .... abdomen .... buttocks .... thighs .... calves .... and toes. .... Feel the total relaxation throughout your body. A calm feeling develops and intensifies..... And you just continue to let go, just letting go more and more.

To help you relax even more, let yourself count slowly from ten to one. You may want to picture yourself going down a long flight of stairs or a long escalator into a place of deeper and deeper comfort and peace, perhaps a lush garden or a spot near a peaceful lake.

[Choose a place that suggests deep peace and comfort to you. Refer directly to it here and in the countdown that follows.]

As each number is called out, see if you can let go and relax a little bit more. Even when it seems impossible to relax any further, there is always that extra bit of calm and relaxation that you can enjoy, simply by letting go more and more..... Ten, relaxing more and more .... nine, even more relaxed .... eight, further and further .... seven, feel that relaxation all over .... six, even more comfortable .... five, halfway there, closer and closer to [your peaceful place] .... four, deeper and still further relaxed .... three, letting go even

more . . . . two, still more relaxed . . . . and one, enjoy the relaxed feelings. . . . . Just continue relaxing like that. . . . .

Continue relaxing like that for a while. . . . .

When you want to stop, slowly stretch your body, breathe
in and out deeply, and gradually get up and resume your normal activities. . . . . Continuing to feel calm and relaxed, yet
wide awake and very alert.

The next exercise is a good one to try after a week or
two of experience with one or more of the other methods.
It is a very quick way to relax and starts the process of
shortening the amount of time required to enter the receptive state you need to accomplish your goals.

Script 4: Rapid Relaxation

Time required: 3 to 4 minutes

When you've found a comfortable position for your body,
take in a really deep breath and fill your lungs. As you are
breathing in, tense every muscle in your body. Hold your breath
in, and study the tension in every part of your body. . . . . Now
exhale, breathe out, and allow your entire body to relax. . . . . Feel
that relief as the relaxation spreads all over and as you let go
more and more. . . . . Do you know just how deeply relaxed you
are? . . . . And do you know just how deeply relaxed you can
be? . . . . Now breathe in again, filling your stomach with air,
and then fill your chest and lungs, and hold it. . . . . And now
let it out slowly. . . . . And then continue to breathe normally
in and out. . . . . Now, as you breathe in, think the word "in,"
and as you breathe out, think the word "out." . . . . Let go of
all your muscles so that you feel pleasantly heavy and calm,
and each time you exhale, feel yourself breathing all the re-
maining tensions out of your body. . . . . Do you know just how
much comfort you can feel? . . . . Now carry on relaxing like
that for just as long as you like. . . . .

Now allow your mind to come up with a word or phrase that describes your present relaxed state. . . . .
[*Use your cue word or phrase here. If by chance you don't already have one, now's the time to come up with it.*]
And say [*your cue word*] to yourself each time you exhale for a moment or two. . . . . You should repeat that word or phrase to yourself whenever you feel this relaxed. The more you do this, the sooner that word or phrase will be able to evoke the feelings whenever you desire.

When you want to stop, just take a deep breath and open your eyes as you exhale. Feel awake, alert, and nicely relaxed. . . . . Remember to stretch your body before getting up, and then slowly stand up and resume your normal activities.

Within a week of daily (or twice-daily) relaxation training, most people get the hang of it and are able to achieve an altered state of consciousness that will enhance their use of the techniques described in the rest of this book.

It is also a good idea to get into the habit of using *differential relaxation*. This refers to the deliberate letting go of those muscles that are not being used at a given time. Thus, if you are sitting and watching TV, there is no need to tense your shoulders, your arms, or the various muscles of your chest and stomach, or your legs. Try to remain as relaxed as you can in many parts of your body while continuing to watch TV (or when looking at any other object, person, scene, or situation). Similarly, if you are writing something, obviously there has to be some tension and activity in the hand and arm you are using, but the other arm and hand do not have to be tense, and nor does your face, most of your stomach muscles, or your legs. Whatever you are doing, try to keep those muscles that are not essential for the job relaxed and loose. For example, if you are standing in line, say at the checkout counter of a supermarket, you will have to tense various muscles in your legs in order to remain standing, but there is really no need to tense your arms and shoulders, or even perhaps your stomach area.

In addition to this differential relaxation, whenever you have a spare moment you can practice relaxing quickly: getting comfortable in your chair, closing your eyes, taking a deep breath or two, and repeating your cue word or imagining your relaxing scene. This exercise can be done anywhere: in a bus, train, or plane; at work or at home; at the movies or opera. The more you do it, the more adept you'll be at relaxing.

Relaxation is a skill, and like any other acquired ability, the more you practice it, the better you'll get at it. If there are particular muscles that remain tense in the exercises, make a new tape that focuses more on them, giving more instructions and taking more time for those muscles to feel pleasantly heavy or light, very loose, very relaxed and comfortable. The main idea is for you to be able to let go of as much tension as possible, so that you are able to employ a wide variety of techniques to their full effect.

Summary: Guidelines for Getting Relaxed

• Unless you already have an effective way of relaxing, read through the four relaxation scripts in this chapter and choose one or several to try out. Feel free to use parts of different exercises to create one relaxation technique that really suits you.

• Have a friend read the exercise to you, or record it yourself on a cassette tape, and then play it back in a quiet setting, doing exactly what the voice on the tape tells you to do. If a friend does read to you the first time or two, you should make a tape of yourself after that or make a tape of the friend reading.

• If you feel more relaxed, more comfortable, after a session, you're doing fine and should play the tape at least once a day for a week or two.

• If you're not more relaxed after the sessions, you need to determine what is wrong and do something about it: try a different exercise, switch to a quieter and more private setting, and so on.

• After you've practiced with the tape for a week or longer, start using briefer techniques as often as you can, preferably more than once each day. Such briefer techniques can include script 4, differential relaxation, or deep breaths and your cue word or relaxing scene.

A CASE OF
STRESS MANAGEMENT

In the next few pages we present an example of stress management using elements of the relaxation techniques in chapter 6 and a few other methods found in later chapters.

A thirty-seven-year-old chemical engineer whom we'll call Harold was suffering from hypertension, intermittent insomnia, gastrointestinal distress, and chronic anxiety. Even more significant was the coronary thrombosis that had virtually incapacitated him for six weeks shortly before his thirty-seventh birthday. He described himself as a "worry-wart," and was given tranquilizers and beta-blockers by his physician. But Harold hated taking pills. "Until recently," he explained, "I seldom took anything more than an occasional vitamin or an aspirin." Despite the pills and despite significant life-style changes — quitting smoking, working less hard, changing his diet, and taking daily walks — he remained a tense, anxious person with persistent high blood pressure and various psychosomatic difficulties.

Harold had been to two psychotherapists with limited success. The first was a psychiatrist who recommended psychoanalytic therapy. "The doctor said I would probably need to see him two or three times a week for several years, but I had neither the time nor the money." Then he saw a psychologist who specialized in biofeedback. "He hooked me up to some machines, and though I was able to relax enough to bring down the tone [of the biofeedback device], I can't say that this proved very effective."

It was immediately apparent that Harold wanted a short-term approach that quickly demonstrated positive results. We decided to try mental training and began by giving him a short speech about its virtues, emphasizing that by dwelling on calm and enjoyable memories, he would constructively alter his physiological processes. "When you picture a pleasant scene and hold it in your mind's eye, your blood pressure comes down, your heart rate slows, your entire body relaxes, and the many benefits of peaceful relaxation are yours to enjoy."

Harold was then asked to get as relaxed as he could in the comfortable chair in which he was sitting, and then to recall a relaxing scene. After a few moments, he was asked to describe it. "I remembered when I was thirteen and went to my uncle's farm in Wyoming during the summer. I had a marvelous time there. While I was sitting here remembering being on the farm, I could literally smell the clean air and hear the animals. It was very peaceful." We asked him to get relaxed and call up the Wyoming farm scene for two to three minutes at a time at least ten times a day for the next week.

When Harold came for his second appointment a week later, he was optimistic. "I used the farm image more than a hundred times this past week. Also, before going to sleep, I pictured myself under one of the trees on the farm, not far from a brook. I was warm and peaceful there and it didn't take long before I dozed off. I got the feeling that this actually improved the quality of my sleep. Is that possible?" We told him that it was indeed quite probable.

We then asked him to come up with three or four additional pleasant and relaxing images so that he could switch back and forth among them. This tends to prevent any particular image from becoming stale. Like so many people, he came up with an ocean scene, "with the breakers gently rolling onto the beach, fleecy clouds in the blue sky, water splashing onto the rocks, and the feeling of warm sun and a cool breeze."

While he was imagining one of his favorite scenes, we provided the following suggestions. Reading them will enable you to see how different parts of the relaxation exercises in the last chapter can be combined, and how repetition is used, to form an effective method for a particular person.

As you sit there like that, feeling relaxed and calm, you are picturing your pleasant scene while listening to my voice. Now I would like you to notice if you feel any warm sensations anywhere in your body. . . . . Allow yourself to keep looking until you notice a warm sensation somewhere in your body. . . . . Good. Now let's take the words "warm, relaxed, and calm" and say them over and over silently to yourself. Warm, relaxed, and calm; warm, relaxed, and calm. Keep on saying those four words over and over to yourself and notice how they induce deeper and deeper levels of tranquility and relaxation. . . . . Warm, relaxed, and calm, very comfortable. Good.

Now to reach a level of even deeper relaxation, to achieve a calm state of profound inner peace, a wonderfully relaxed and calm state of mind and body, just continue sitting like that, keeping your eyes closed, and think of yourself breathing tension out of your body each time you exhale. As you breathe out, more and more tension leaves your body, so that you feel deeper and deeper levels of relaxation. . . . . Now again, hear the words "warm, relaxed, and calm." . . . . Very good.

Whenever you desire to reach your present state of altered consciousness, when you wish to feel deeply and profoundly relaxed, all you have to do is sit down, relax, close your eyes, and repeat those three words — "warm, relaxed, and calm" — to yourself over and over for a minute or so. Wherever you are, whatever you're doing, when you want to feel as you do now, just sit down, get comfortable, close your eyes, and repeat your cue words — "warm, relaxed, and calm" — over and over to yourself for a minute or two, allowing yourself to feel the spreading warmth, calmness, and comfort. Excellent. . . . .

Now I'm going to count backwards from five to one. When I reach two, open your eyes and feel relaxed, but quite fresh, alert, and wide awake. Five, four, three, two, open your eyes, and one. . . . . How do you feel?

Harold stated that he had achieved a level of extremely deep comfort: "I just broke the tension barrier!" We asked him to continue practicing his relaxing imagery at home plus the cue words "warm, relaxed, and calm."

We then devoted several sessions to helping apply his new skills to stressful situations. Harold drew up a list of situations that he found difficult to deal with, circumstances that invariably elevated his blood pressure further. Then, starting with the easiest item on the list, we had him imagine handling it in a better way.

One item on the easier end of the list was getting upset when colleagues came late for a meeting. We asked him to imagine anticipating their lateness and bringing some work or reading material to the meeting, so he would have something to do while he waited for the latecomers. Then —

in a relaxed state, of course — we had him imagine himself in the meeting room, doing his work or reading his paper, feeling fittingly indifferent to what others did. His attitude was expressed in the following words, which he often repeated to himself in his imagery work: "If they choose to be late, it's their business. It's their lives and I will not let their behavior get to me." This is a good example of *process imagery,* imagining exactly how he was going to handle the situation, and *direct suggestion* — "I will not let their behavior get to me."

A more difficult item was reflected in this statement: "I can't cope when the phones are ringing, when the office is noisy with everyone shouting at everyone else, and I have five things to attend to." You can almost feel his anxiety as you read the words.

The first thing we taught Harold was the importance of not trying to do five things at once. There is only one reasonable way to do things and that is one at a time. Yes, you may have five projects underway or five reports due at the end of the month, but you can only work fruitfully on one at a time. And as you work on that one, that's all you should be doing. When you finish, or need a break, you can turn to something else, where the same rules apply. You then focus only on that report or item. We had Harold imagine doing just this: pushing everything else aside and working on only one thing. He felt immensely relieved about being able to work on only one thing, but then asked what to do if while he was working on project A someone called with a question or comment about project C. We agreed that most times he didn't have to take the call. He could return it later when he was working on project C or have the other party call back at that time. We had him imagine not taking calls. Again he felt great relief. It's a good feeling to be able to deal with one thing at a time and not be constantly interrupted.

As Harold practiced imagining how he would handle this situation, he also started handling it this way in the office and was delighted by the results. We had planned to do some work with him to help him ignore the noise in the office, but it turned out to be unnecessary. As Harold developed his powers of concentration, just focusing on the one matter in front of him, he was less and less aware of what was going on in the rest of the room. Occasionally things threatened to get out of hand, but Harold used the same procedure he used to deal with people coming late to meetings. He just told himself to do his work as best he could. If others got twisted in knots and yelled, that was their problem, their lives. He could take pride in the fact that he was not like them and didn't have to act crazy. Their behavior wasn't going to get to him, and by and large it didn't.

In less than three months, Harold was able to stop taking his medicine. His blood pressure was within normal limits and he stated that he was feeling well physically and "infinitely calmer" emotionally. "Things that used to get me all worked up," he volunteered, "hardly bother me anymore. I have developed a very different outlook." We urged him to continue with his dietary changes, exercise regimen, and other health-related activities, and to be sure to use his imagery and self-calming statements daily. A follow-up interview after eight months revealed he had maintained his gains. "I use self-hypnosis and imagery the way a diabetic uses insulin," he said. "As long as I use these methods, I'm fine. A couple of months ago I got lazy and stopped my physical and psychological exercises, and I began to experience the same old problems. That was a real test for me. It proved that these methods really work and it's not all in my mind." But it is, Harold, it really is.

We have used similar methods with equal success with many people. Among them are a number of women who developed stress-related symptoms as a result of trying to juggle a job or career, children, finances, and housework, often without a mate or with one who wanted more than he gave. While it wouldn't be true or fair to say that it's all in their heads, helping these women relax and change their thoughts and images usually resulted in significant changes in their lives.

The mind of man is capable of anything because everything is in it.

— Joseph Conrad

CHAPTER 7

RECALLING PAST SUCCESSES

We all have within us the key to feeling stronger, more confident, more resourceful, and more successful. By recalling and focusing on times when you were successful, you recreate the feelings of confidence, power, and accomplishment that are associated with these successes, and that helps to ensure good feelings and positive results in the present and future. Recollection of past achievements is one of the most powerful kinds of imagery available to anyone.

All of us have been successful and effective at something, but it's amazing how quickly we forget or minimize these experiences. This is unfortunate because the memories of what we succeeded at in the past can increase the probability of our doing well now. And please don't say your successes are too trivial for consideration. Remember the story of Charles Schulz in chapter 3. The only thing he had been successful at was drawing and "coining little phrases," but that was enough.

It may be true that you never sold computers before,

but you did very well selling cars and appliances. It may be true that you never had to deal with the kind of brilliant and brash entrepreneurs now confronting you, but you did deal effectively with equally brash and brilliant corporate executives before. It may be true that you never before competed in the Olympics, but you did compete in and win a number of regional and national events.

It's terrific if your past successes were in situations similar to the one you're facing, although that can't always be. But success in any situation can be used. You have almost certainly done some things well. Maybe you once gave a good talk, did well in a play or in a sport, were very helpful to a friend in sorting out a problem, organized some kind of sale or other event, gave advice that proved useful to a colleague, or gave up smoking. If you have trouble coming up with these experiences, recall some things you were complimented for. The memories of any one or several of these experiences can be used to make you more effective in the situation you're now facing.

Because of family connections, a client of ours was given the job of rescuing a small company (which we'll call Freeman Widget Company) from the brink of bankruptcy even though she had no prior business experience. Suzie had been a college professor and had never given much thought to money or business. When she came to us she was overwhelmed by the strange world of business and law that she had inhabited for less than two months. She was close to saying that she had made a mistake in taking the job and would have to bail out. After all, she said, she didn't know the first thing about finance, manufacturing, or bankruptcy, and she absolutely despised lawyers and everything having to do with the legal system.

After she calmed down, Suzie said there was another side of her, the side that loved challenges, the side that would love to do well in her job. But she was feeling overwhelmed and terrified. Nothing in her training or profession had prepared her for this job and she had nothing to fall back on.

But hadn't she, we asked, done well in other difficult, seemingly impossible, situations? Suzie said she had and told us about them, but she couldn't see their relevance. We explained that the relevance was not in content, but simply in the fact of prevailing in difficult circumstances. We asked her to recall one of the past situations and her feelings at the beginning: the excitement of the challenge and the fear of failure (not much different from what she was feeling now). She did so and we gave a few suggestions. Just as she had used the strong emotions in the earlier situation to summon the best in her, so she would do the same in the present. Just as she had dealt with each obstacle in turn, overcoming each until she finally prevailed, so too she would do so in the present. In the four months we saw Suzie, such suggestions were frequently given and she gave them to herself at home and in her office.

Suzie really was ignorant about many crucial matters and there wasn't time for her to take courses to improve her knowledge. But although she didn't at first see its relevance, she had been an effective administrator in a number of situations. Since her current position required someone who could gather and use the information of others — an administrator — we were able to use her past successes to help in the effort. We gave suggestions along these lines:

> Just as you were able to use the political knowledge of X [a person in a department she once headed], the money-juggling skills of Y, and the diplomatic adroitness of Z in your work at the college, so too you'll be able to make effective use of the resources and knowledge of those at Freeman Widget. Recall how you felt

when you first asked X how best to approach the dean about the NSF grants. . . . . Good. And now recall how you used his knowledge. Recall how well it all worked out, his telling you who needed to be approached by whom and how, and how you made use of the information. . . . . Remember how wonderful you felt when you got what you wanted. And now imagine how you'll use someone in the current job the same way. . . . . Just as you were able to use the skills and knowledge of X and Y and Z at the school, so too you'll be able to use the skills and knowledge of other people at Freeman Widget. And imagine how good you'll feel when the company is in good shape and you've triumphed once more.

Suzie was a remarkably talented woman who had all kinds of relevant successes we were able to use. When she felt nervous before making a presentation to her board on a topic about which she didn't feel knowledgeable enough, we had her search her memory for any related experiences. Sure enough, there were a number of them. Most people have had to make presentations they felt unprepared to make. We asked her to pick the one that felt most appropriate to the situation and go over it in her mind in detail, recalling all the feelings and especially how effective she had been. We then gave the familiar suggestion that her talk at the board meeting next week would go the same way and have similar results.

The job required that Suzie deal with lawyers and legal matters, and there was no getting around this. Somehow she would have to overcome what almost amounted to a phobia. Two kinds of aid were used. When we used the word *phobia,* Suzie volunteered that as a child she had been terribly afraid of dogs but had been able to overcome the fear on her own. We used this information about the successful resolution of a past fear to give her hope that she could do the same now with a different fear.

We also discovered that Suzie greatly admired Abraham Lincoln, viewing him as plain and unimpressive on the outside but very savvy, very tough, and quite manipulative on the inside — much as she saw herself. We had her use the model technique (about which we say more in interlude 3): Lincoln — himself a lawyer, an irony not lost on Suzie or us — became her adviser on dealing with lawyers and also her model of how to do it. After imagining many times how Abe, as she called him, would have the kind of discussion she needed to have with Freeman Widget's lawyers, she began to feel that she might be able to have that kind of discussion. Gradually, she practiced having that discussion until she actually was able to do it. Not totally calm and confident, but close enough so that she achieved her goals. Just as she could overcome her fear of dogs in the past, so she could overcome her fear of lawyers in the present. And she did just that.

There are three main ways to use past successes. First, if you have trouble relaxing, and especially if you are made more tense by trying to relax, you should recall past successes in place of relaxation. Simply remember a past success whenever we say to get relaxed. Second, if relaxation is easy, you should use the powerful image of a past success, and the feelings associated with it, immediately after getting relaxed and before commencing with goal or process imagery. This procedure helps set a positive and confident tone for what comes next. And third, everyone should build recollection of past successes into their goal and process imagery, just as we did with Suzie. Whenever you need a boost of confidence or strength, recall a time when you felt confident and strong. These memories also become a kind of posthypnotic suggestion (a subject we discuss in chapter 11). The word pattern we used with

Suzie — "Just as you succeeded with X, so now you will succeed with Y" — is one standard structure for posthypnotic cues.

Your success images should be as intense as possible. To make them more powerful, experiment with their structure (as discussed on pages 78–83). If you're viewing them from a separated perspective, try merging into them and see what that does. Whether they are separated or merged images, make the pictures larger and clearer. Dramatic music can make a big difference, so hum or recall something from Beethoven's Ninth Symphony, Wagner, *Chariots of Fire,* or anything else that inspires you.

After you are relaxed — or instead of being relaxed, if you are someone for whom relaxation is difficult — play a tape that you've already made with instructions similar to what follows in script 5.

Script 5: Recalling a Past Success

Time required: 4 to 7 minutes

As you sit there feeling pleasantly relaxed, allow your mind to go back, as far back as it needs, to recall a successful experience, a time when you felt very strong, very good about yourself, very pleased with your accomplishment. Doesn't make any difference what the experience was. Might be something big, might be something small. Might be something others knew about, might be something only you knew about. Doesn't really make any difference. The only important thing is that you felt successful and were proud of yourself. . . . . When that experience comes up, get into it as deeply as possible. Where were you? What were you wearing? Exactly what did you do? Recall it as vividly as you can, as if you are reliving the experience. . . . . Good. And now recall the feelings you had at the time. . . . . The sense of power, of accomplishment, the confi-

dence, the pride. . . . . Feels good, doesn't it? . . . . Stay with those feelings a while longer. . . . .

Would you like to feel them again, to have more experiences where you are successful and feel as strong, as sure, as confident? You can, you know.

[*In the following sentence, where we use conquering a fear of dogs and gaining confidence around lawyers, substitute a description of one of your past successes and one of your present goals. Continue to use these where appropriate in the rest of the paragraph.*]

Just as you succeeded and felt great when you overcame your fear of dogs, so you can succeed in doing business with the lawyers and feel great about it. Just as you've reached goals in the past, you'll reach goals in the future. Just as you learned to be confident and comfortable with dogs as a child — a huge and wonderful achievement for a little girl — so you'll learn to be confident and comfortable with lawyers.

Now let's do that again with another successful experience. [*Use another successful experience or another time when you felt very good about yourself. Refer to that experience by name or detail it where appropriate throughout this paragraph and in the one that follows, and substitute one of your present goals in the last sentence of the next paragraph.*]

Recall another time you achieved your goal and felt very positive, very strong, very proud. . . . . Recall it as clearly as you can, all the important details. . . . . Very good. And recall how you felt, how confident and powerful and proud, how terrific it felt to be you. . . . . Just as you felt that good then, you can feel that good again. Isn't it great to feel good?

Recalling past accomplishments and successes is very important for you, and you should recall one or two several times each day, along with the wonderful feelings that accompanied them. The more you recall past successes, the better you'll feel. The more you recall past successes, the stronger, more confident, and more resourceful you'll feel and know yourself to be. The more you recall past successes, the more successes you'll have. Just as you succeeded in getting the NSF grant at the university and felt great about it, so you'll succeed in getting the backing you need for the company and feel great about that.

The more you recall past successes and how wonderful you felt, the more you'll succeed in the future and feel even better.

Stay with the terrific feelings as long as you want. . . . . When you're ready, slowly return to your everyday consciousness any way you want, taking the strong feelings with you, feeling alert, powerful, and ready to go to it.

Your past successes are already part of you and represent a resource of immense power and effectiveness, one frequently and unfortunately left untapped. Why not use them to help in the present? They don't require much in the way of time and energy to recall and the rewards can be huge. Use what you've got.

We are what we imagine ourselves to be.
    — *Kurt Vonnegut, Jr.*

CHAPTER 8

IMAGINING THE RESULTS

There are two basic types of imagery used in mental training, aside from the relaxing imagery and recalling of past successes already discussed. In one type, *result* or *goal imagery*, you imagine already having achieved the outcome you desire — for instance, being a confident and effective public speaker, being more productive, having more relaxed and constructive conversations with your mate, or feeling more comfort and less pain in your life. In the other type, *process imagery*, you imagine the means by which you will accomplish the result.

To put the differences in a nutshell, in result imagery you imagine how you'd feel after you've baked a cake, with the accomplishment behind you. In process imagery, you imagine yourself, step by step, baking the cake. An example from Jack Nicklaus's *Golf My Way* shows how sophisticated these two kinds of imagery can be in combination:

I never hit a shot without having a very sharp, in-focus picture of it in my head. It's like a color movie.

First I "see" the ball where I want it to finish, nice and white and sitting up high on the bright green grass [one type of result imagery]. Then the scene quickly changes and I "see" the ball going there: its path, trajectory, and shape, even its behavior on landing [another example of goal imagery]. Then there's a sort of fade-out, and the next scene shows me making the kind of swing that will turn the previous images into reality [process imagery].

These two types of imagery are essential in any mental-training program, regardless of the specific goals or means to them. This chapter is devoted to result imagery, while the next one deals with process imagery. There are three reasons for putting the end before the means. First, regularly fantasizing about what life will be like after you've achieved your goal will help you to do what is necessary to make the changes you desire. In short, it will motivate you. This is of crucial importance. Having a goal regularly in mind gets you going in the right direction and keeps you headed that way.

Second, regularly fantasizing about your goal will help you start thinking about yourself in a new way, and this new self-perception or identity will prepare you for the change and help make it happen. Our identities are important in contributing a sense of continuity and cohesiveness to our lives. But they also become obstacles to change. If statements such as "I'm not outgoing," "I'm not good at math," and "I don't take well to new ideas" are part of your identity, you are limiting what is possible for you. It will be hard to be convivial, it will be hard to learn math or deal with numbers, and it will be hard to understand or accept new ideas. But if you change these parts of your identity, you'll have a much easier time of it.

Result imagery gives you opportunities to play with your

identity, to explore what it would be like to feel and act and be different. In the process, it combats the negative hypnosis you've been performing on yourself. Instead of always imagining yourself as failing, say, at math, you have a chance to imagine what it would be like to be good at math. You can also see what it's like to imagine yourself as confident, assertive, and successful. Trying on new identities can open many doors.

There is yet a third reason for putting result imagery before process imagery. It's hard to get somewhere if you don't know where you want to go. Jack Nicklaus puts the idea succinctly: "Visualizing the swing is useless if you fail to visualize what it's supposed to achieve." Thomas Watson, Sr., was once asked when he first envisioned IBM becoming so big. His answer was, "Right at the beginning." Charles Garfield reports in his study of peak performers in American business: "As early as 1924, when [Watson] changed the name of the Computing-Tabulating-Recording Company to International Business Machines, he envisioned what IBM would look like as a big, mature business (when it was 'done,' as he put it). Then every day he worked to correct the difference between the objective and the present path."

Goal imagery has a lot in common with what actors do. Take a woman who is going to play the queen of England. Of course she isn't the queen and isn't likely to be. But for her to play her role successfully, she has to act as if she were indeed the queen. And she does it by using her imagination, just as you can use yours. She goes over in her mind, time and again, being the queen. The more she does it, the more she becomes the queen. Not, mind you, Sally Smith playing the queen, but the real queen. When the imagination has been given enough practice in taking the part of the queen, what comes out is not "Well, I wonder what the queen would have done in this situation," but rather "I am the queen and I need to do something about this business of the Spanish Armada." Similarly, if you imagine often enough being successful, productive, comfortable, and so on, you will start acting as if that is really what you are.

Unfortunately, some people are offended by the idea of goal imagery. It sounds like wishful thinking to them, as if simply imagining being thin will make a person thin. In response to such objections, there are several points worth making. Imaging is not the same as wishful thinking. To the contrary, it is enlisting the powerful resources of human imagination in systematic and proven ways to achieve certain ends.

Critics of the use of imagery also assume that goal or result imagery is all that is required to bring about change through mental training. As we stated earlier, most people require a combination of several or all of the methods in this book. One of the great benefits of result imagery is that it helps you determine what else you need to do to accomplish your goals, and it motivates you to do those things.

One final response to critics of imagery is that they miss the subtlety and therefore the power of the method. When you regularly imagine having achieved your goal, you are changing who you are. You are, to take the example of losing weight, getting used to thinking and feeling as a thin person. You can actually feel what it's like to buy clothes with joy and without embarrassment. You can actually imagine yourself having a great time at the beach or pool. In these ways, you are changing your view of yourself, changing your identity from that of a fat person to that of a thin person. The new view and new identity will make it more possible for you actually to become the person you fantasize about.

The above responses to critics of goal imagery are the main reasons we use it. There is one more, which by this time seems almost needless to say: It works.

To use result imagery, it is necessary to define as precisely as you can what goal(s) you wish to achieve. We assume you have already done this, but if not, there's no time like the present. If you've already defined your goals using the exercises in chapter 4, now is a good time to look at them again and see if you want to make changes or if you can make them more specific. If you want to be thinner, you need to decide by how many pounds or how you would look in, say, a swimsuit. If you want to be more productive, you need some measure of how much more. If you're a writer who usually turns out ten pages a day, perhaps you want to produce fifteen pages a day. If you're depressed, maybe one goal is to spend more time with friends and another is to accept some of the social invitations you receive. If you're shy, perhaps one of your goals is to start a conversation with the man or woman down the hall. Whatever it is you want to accomplish, you need a clear and specific criterion.

Once you have your goals, the procedure is quite simple. You will get relaxed and, using taped instructions you'll prepare beforehand, imagine yourself already having achieved the goal. In your mind's eye, you'll be a person who's given many well-received public talks, who is known as a good communicator, who has been complimented many times for skill in negotiation or assertiveness, whose ability to do such and such (your goal) is much admired by others, or who is known for being well organized.

Here are some of the ways Ann, a real-estate agent, used result imagery to improve her productivity and comfort. Before using mental training, she was having a terrible time in her work. Her sales were below the average at her office, she felt a sense of dread when she went to work, and she was ridden with anxiety when she called clients or took them to see a house. She wanted to feel more comfortable at selling and to sell more. Her ultimate goal was to be one of the top three agents in her office. As for her mission, it was clear and simple: "I want the money but that's secondary. I mainly want to prove to myself and my family that I can be very good at what I do."

In Ann's office, productivity is indicated on a bulletin board, where every quarter the agents are listed from top to bottom according to their sales. An image that captured her long-term goal was going to the bulletin board and seeing her name in one of the top three places. We had her use the image from the start, to remind her of what she wanted and how good it would feel knowing she was one of the best in her office. We also went a step farther — so far that Ann could only giggle when she first tried it. We had her fantasize being on a vacation in Mexico with her husband, her reward for being the top agent in her office for the year. Despite her initial discomfort, she practiced the image regularly and became more comfortable with it as she did.

As we review the result imagery Ann used, it's important that you keep in mind that this imagery was only part of the program she followed to develop her resources; she also used many of the other techniques that we discuss in this book. One of Ann's favorite images, which she used throughout her work with us, was of talking confidently on the phone with a prospective buyer, setting up an appointment to show him a property. Over and over she imagined herself feeling peaceful and strong while talking to the client and heard these qualities reflected in her words and her tone of voice. As she mastered this part of the imagery, she added a new part: getting compliments about her manner and confidence from two agents in her office who overheard the conversation. She imagined how good she would feel receiving their words of praise and how nice it was to feel not only accepted but even admired by the other agents.

Writing contracts is an essential part of real-estate work

but one Ann thought she did poorly. She was never sure if her wording was as binding and precise as it should be, never sure if it would stand up to legal scrutiny, a concern she shares with many Realtors. She got very anxious when it came to drawing up contracts and would pester other agents in the office for advice on almost every point. On this matter, it was important for Ann to gain more knowledge about contract writing, but she was not enthusiastic when we recommended taking a course or getting consultation.

But Ann realized she would never feel good about her work until she mastered the art of writing good contracts. When asked her goals in this area, she said she would like to become so good at contracts that she regularly produced the best possible and, in an interesting turn of events, that other agents would turn to her for help.

Three images embodied these goals and Ann used all three of them. In the first, she imagined how good she would feel having just finished a very complicated contract, knowing that no one could have done better. In the second, she saw herself being consulted by a very experienced agent for help with a contract he was writing. And in the third, she imagined her client, a lawyer, complimenting her on the fine contract she had just written for his purchase of a home, saying, "I didn't know anyone but a lawyer could write such a good contract." Ann liked the feelings she had when focusing on these images and before long arranged for a series of consultations on contract writing with a real-estate attorney.

It is significant that Ann at first resisted the idea of consultation or courses to improve her contracts. Only after using the imagery and realizing how much she would like to be good in this area of her work did she feel motivated to acquire the necessary knowledge.

Ann also needed help in dealing with what she called

"lookers only," clients who wanted to look at every property on the market but who never bought. They would take up a great deal of her time and energy. She drove them from one place to another and often got involved in long discussions about the pros and cons of this and that home, and sometimes even in drawing up contracts, but always they would find a reason why the property was not quite right and want to look some more. Other agents found it easier to dump such clients or at least not spend so much time with them, but Ann felt guilty when contemplating these options. She suspected that it was really her fault. If she had shown them more appropriate places or had made a better sales pitch, they would have bought. At the same time, however, she envied agents who didn't get so involved with such clients and who spent their time with people serious about buying.

Ann needed to deal with her guilt and to learn some things about being more assertive, which she did, but it was the result imagery that carried her through. The technique of using a model (which we discuss in interlude 3) proved helpful. Ann very much admired the ways a younger but more experienced agent, Sandy, handled her "lookers." We had Ann imagine handling these clients the way Sandy did, even saying the words Sandy used. (This is process imagery, which we discuss in the next chapter.)

We also asked her to imagine how good she would feel after getting rid of one of these clients or limiting the time she spent with one of them. Ann was surprised at how relieved she felt. She hadn't before realized exactly how much energy these clients were consuming and how angry she was at them. Her comment was, "No wonder Sandy is usually in such a good mood while I'm usually feeling like I've been run over by a train."

As Ann had more experience thinking of herself as helpful and effective, she realized the problem was in the lookers and not in herself. She also realized that a confident, effective Realtor would not endlessly cater to the lookers' needs. As she saw herself as more and more successful, she had less need to put up with impossible clients. A statement she made near the end of her therapy about one such couple is worth repeating, for it clearly indicates the change in her self-perception: "I'm a good Realtor and I've busted my buns for them. I've shown them at least ten houses that were suitable and affordable. I get the feeling that nothing will satisfy them and they'll still be looking long after I've retired. I'm not willing to spend any more time chauffeuring them around."

Ann continued her work with us for several months, changing the focus and the imagery as her confidence and skills developed. But several images were used throughout, one of them being her becoming a top seller at the office. As she developed her skills and comfort, she used this image more and more. The more she imagined it, the more she realized how much she wanted it. The images of seeing her name in one of the top three spots on the bulletin board and winning the vacation in Mexico spurred her on. Within a year and a half after beginning her work with us, long after she had ended her therapy, Ann achieved her first goal. She was number three in sales. Two years later, she won her vacation.

Ann's success illustrates most of the points we made at the beginning of this chapter. There was no magic involved but rather a lot of hard work systematically aimed at reaching her goals. The result imagery was important for two main reasons. As we have indicated several times, it helped motivate her to pursue the means by which her goals could be achieved; for instance, getting consultation so that she could better understand and write contracts. The result imagery also helped change her view of herself.

At the beginning, she saw herself as not quite a competent Realtor: unsure of herself in many ways, lacking confidence and knowledge, uncomfortable with many aspects of her work, and often needing the help of others in her office. She was heavily involved in the negative hypnosis and performance anxiety so common to people in her situation. For instance, when a new client was referred to her, she immediately told herself that she wouldn't do well by the new prospect, that he probably wouldn't like her, that even if she found an appropriate property she would probably screw up the contract, and it would all end with the client finding a better Realtor and the referral source being dissatisfied with her. Given all this, it's no wonder she was anxious and not doing well.

The result imagery helped her see herself in a new way. It gave her practice feeling competent, confident, and helpful. She liked these feelings, as does almost everyone, and started to believe that she was entitled to have them. Slowly but surely, her identity changed. The imagery gave her the experience of being successful. Even though it was only in her head, she started feeling more successful and that, as most successful people will tell you, is half the battle. She gradually felt more confident when clients called, when she showed them properties, and when she drew up contracts.

Below is the basic result imagery exercise that Ann used and that you can use. Regardless of your goal, you should employ goal imagery, using it before any other imagery and throughout your program.

Before you do the exercise, spend a few minutes coming up with several images that embody the achievement of your goals. For example, you're not planning to make more money, you've already made it. You're not trying to be more confident, you already are. You're not trying to feel more comfort and less pain in your body, you already feel that way. Imagine yourself being applauded, being handed the trophy or award, producing or having produced whatever it is you want to produce. Make the images as powerful as possible by changing their structure. The award should be large, the applause very loud, and everything close, clearly defined, and brightly lit. There should also be action (like Ann's walking up to the bulletin board and seeing her name near the top of the list). Once again we remind you of the importance of playing some music in your mind that enhances your feelings of strength and accomplishment as you listen to your tape.

Before recording the goal imagery on the tape, include enough relaxation instructions to get yourself comfortably relaxed. Use whatever you've found helpful from your own experience or from our relaxation scripts. Give plenty of detail to help yourself get deeply involved with the result imagery and be sure to include a lot of positive reinforcement in the recording ("fine," "that's good," "terrific," and so on).

Our script is based on several made for a woman whose goal was weight loss and involves more scenes than should be used at the beginning. There are actually seven separate scenes here. We are using them all at once only to give you an idea of the possibilities. For your own tape, use only one or two scenes; for example, looking in the mirror and walking down the hallway. You will need to make changes that reflect your particular goals, your personality, your interests, your situation. Even if your goal is weight loss, you will probably still have to make changes to make the tape suit you. The woman for whom this tape was made was extremely concerned about her looks and how other people responded to her body. These were her primary interests, not ours, but our words reflect her situation, down to the last detail. In our list of body parts to look at in the mirror, we used the parts she had expressed concern about. Other people who want to lose weight may be more concerned about their general health, for example, rather than their looks, and their imagery should reflect that interest. With our client, it would have done no good at all to ask her to imagine what a clean bill of health she'd get next time she saw her doctor. She didn't care much about that. Just as we tried to use what would motivate her, you should use what will motivate you.

Script 6: Result Imagery

Time required: 5 to 7 minutes for one or two scenes

Now that you are peacefully relaxing, it would be nice to use your imagination. As you do so, you can continue to relax even further and deeper, very comforting relaxation. . . . . Can you imagine that you're already down to 120 pounds, that you've already lost all the weight you want to lose? . . . . Imagine looking at your thinner self in your bedroom mirror. Take a good, long look, starting with your toes, up your legs, and yes, be sure to look at your thighs and hips, now so feminine, the way you wanted for so long, now so pleasing to look at. . . . . Turn sideways and get another angle. Very nice, isn't it? . . . . And now turn your back to the mirror for another view. . . . . Not too shabby. . . . . And face the mirror again and make sure you see your stomach, your breasts, and your much slimmer arms and neck. . . . . Quite pleasing, wouldn't you say? Imagine how terrific you feel, looking like this, how feminine, how presentable, how good it feels to look like this. . . . .

Keeping those good feelings, imagine how you'd look in a summer dress, walking down the hallway at work. . . . . Imagine running into Stan in the hallway, how good you'd feel. . . . . And now Jean and Sylvia come up to join you. Suddenly you realize that you're as slender as Jean. Isn't that a great feeling? . . . . Good. Let's leave the hallway and go shopping.

Can you imagine how this thinner you feels when shopping

for an outfit at Saks? . . . . That's right, imagine the whole process, looking at the size-nine racks. . . . . Can you imagine that, you looking at size nines for the first time in twenty years? Doesn't that feel great? . . . . Seeing how fashionable the clothes are . . . . taking several into the dressing room . . . . and feeling so proud and content as you look at yourself in the mirror after you've removed your dress. . . . . And trying on the new clothes, one outfit at a time. . . . . Imagine the looks of approval you get from the salespeople. . . . . Imagine how proud you feel as you pay for it. . . . . Imagine how you look as you wear your new outfit the first time. . . . . Excellent, and now just let that image fade away. . . . .

Now, can you imagine what your mother says when she sees the new you for the first time? . . . . Can you see the pride in her eyes and hear it in her voice? . . . . And how good that makes you feel? Good, and let that fade away. . . . .

Now imagine looking at a newspaper ad for a weight-reduction program or a fat-farm and suddenly realizing the ads have nothing to do with you. . . . . And now imagine seeing an ad on TV for the newest diet or diet pill and realizing that it is totally irrelevant to you. . . . . Doesn't that make you feel on top of the world? . . . . That's good and let it go. . . . . And continue to relax, calm and at ease. . . . . You're doing fine.

Can you imagine the new, thin you lying on the beach in an absolutely smashing bikini, bright red and very skimpy? You deserve it, so imagine it as vividly as you can. . . . . And make sure to imagine all the attention you receive from both women and men, especially that blond guy you've been eyeing for the last half hour. . . . . Not that you're going to do anything with him, of course, but the attention is nice. Very good. And let it fade away. . . . .

One more image, one you're sure to enjoy. Can you imagine being in bed with Nick, very proud of your body, showing it off at every opportunity, with no more fear, no more concern that he'll be turned off by the folds of flab, no more twisting and turning to present the slimmest side of you, just pride and anticipation? .... Imagine the new, svelte you, imagine him appreciating and approving..... What does he say as his hands caress your now flat tummy? .... Imagine how you feel when his hands move down your now slim thighs, you feeling only pride and enjoyment...., Let yourself go and imagine the fun, the excitement, the growing pleasure..... Nothing to hide, everything to show off..... Enjoy the scene for as long as you like, and then let it go..... That's very good, you're doing fine.

When you're ready, take a deep breath, hold it a second, and as you exhale, open your eyes and feel fully alert, fully awake, fully functioning, with the certain knowledge that you're on the right road to reach your goals.

If you absolutely can't imagine yourself accomplishing your goals, rely on a fantasy of someone you admire, whether or not you actually know the person (the model technique in interlude 3).

Another thing to check if you have trouble with this exercise is whether your goals are too vague. If they are, you'll definitely have trouble imagining their realization. Use the material in chapter 4 to focus more specifically on what you want.

One problem with result imagery is that some people get frightened by imaging having reached their goals. To take but one example, a few people we've worked with got upset when imagining being thinner. Suddenly they realized, for instance, that being slimmer would mean they'd have to deal with sex, something their fat had protected them from for a long time. If that's the case — and we emphasize that it is for only a very small number of people — we suggest putting the goal aside for the moment and replacing it with achieving more comfort with the problematic issue. To continue with the example of fear of sex, we would have you make a list of sexual behaviors, from the least anxiety-arousing to the most. After getting deeply relaxed, you should imagine engaging in the least fearful activity. When you're completely comfortable with that, you should go on to the next image, and so forth until you're comfortable with all the items on the list. Obviously this process can take days, weeks, or even longer and is best done with tapes. After the thought of having sex no longer arouses anxiety, you can return to imagining a slimmer, more sexy self.

Listen to your goal imagery tape twice a day for a week or two (which means anywhere from ten to fifteen minutes a day, depending on how long your tape is). When you can clearly imagine various parts of it without the tape, then do just that for ten to fifteen minutes a day for another week or two. After that, take a minute or two every day to imagine having achieved your goal. The best way to reduce the amount of time is simply to use only a part of your original tape. Just a quick look in the mirror at the new you or just a glance at yourself at the size-nine rack in the store. Explore every aspect and facet of the new, successful you. After several weeks of work with goal imagery, you should be able to do it very quickly. Whenever you have a spare moment or two, use your quick route to relaxation and then, just as quickly, imagine one example of your having achieved your goals.

Summary: Guidelines for Imagining the Goals

• Choose a number of images that embody the achievement of your goals. Remember that the images should reflect you after you've achieved them.
• Use the images as much as possible, but mainly when you are relaxed. Do at least ten to fifteen minutes of im-

agery work every day, using tapes of your own making for at least the first two weeks. After that, you can quickly imagine one part of your success imagery without a tape.

• One or more of the long-range goals can be imagined from the start as a way of keeping your goal in sight and motivating you to do whatever else is required. But most of your imagery should be of what you are working on right now (like Ann's seeing herself writing better contracts).

• Especially on the tapes, but at other times as well, compliment and congratulate yourself on what you're doing. Give lots of "you're doing fine," "very good," and similar statements. You deserve them. Successful people are generally not averse to giving themselves credit.

THREE OPTIONAL EXERCISES

In this interlude we provide three additional exercises. Though none of them is necessary for effective mental training, all have been helpful to many people. Each is easy to learn and can be used with the techniques in later chapters. They are also fun for many people, evoking their creativity and playfulness.

A Room of Your Own

Getting relaxed is a way of being in a different state than you are usually in. Some people, as we have seen, go to a specific relaxing place such as a beach or meadow. There is a way of going even further with this: constructing a special room of your own, exactly the way you want it to be, with the layout, colors, and furnishings exactly as you like.

This then becomes your very own special place, totally private unless you decide to tell someone about it or invite someone to go there with you, a sanctuary that you can visit any time you wish. When you need a refuge, when you need a place to recharge yourself, to lick your wounds, to get yourself together, to go and think — whenever you need a place for any of these or any other reasons, you can quickly and easily go there.

June, gifted with a very talented and very active imagination, immediately took to the idea of a room of her own. She found it enticing that the room was hers to do with as she liked. Her room became all things to her — one of them, of course, being a place to relax. June loved nature and decided she could have whatever natural vistas she desired. Sometimes she would be in an ocean mood. She'd look out the window of her room and see a vast expanse of ocean, with waves breaking on the shore and sailing boats close in, with larger ships farther out. At other times, she'd be in a jungle mood and would look out on lush vegetation, hearing the sounds of various animals.

Perhaps most important, June's place became her Office of Strategic Planning. Here she mulled over important questions such as whether she should stay with her husband, whether to continue in her present work, and what to do about some projects she had left half-finished for years. She had, of course, considered these questions before. But now it was different. "In my room," she said, "I think much more clearly. I have a better sense of who I am and what's right for me. I'm in touch not only with my thoughts but also with my deeper, intuitive side. I can concentrate for much longer periods of time because, when I get tired, I just gaze out on my scene for the day and become replenished. Then back to my planning."

By now you should be familiar with the basic plan. Make a tape starting with enough relaxation suggestions to allow you to be comfortably relaxed. Then record the following script, or a variation of it.

Script 7: A Room of Your Own

Time required: 3 to 5 minutes

As you sit there feeling very calm and very much at ease, allow your mind, in its own way and at its own pace, to suggest a very, very special place, very safe and private, a room of your very own, unknown to anyone but you, a place you can arrange any way you like and that you can go to whenever you want to do whatever you wish. A room of your own, where you can be totally yourself. . . . . Where you can relax. . . . . Where you can get in touch with inner resources. . . . . Where you can be aware of your goodness and strengths. . . . . Where you can mull things over if you like. . . . . Where you can determine what's in your best interests. . . . . Where you can plan changes you want to make. . . . . Where you can do anything at all that you want to do at that moment. . . . . You deserve this kind of place, so just allow your mind to suggest the right kind of very, very special place for yourself. Take your time. . . . . When you have a place in mind, try it out. Mentally walk around it. . . . . Look out the window, if it has one. . . . . Check out the feel and smell and sounds of it. . . . . See if it's right for you and, remembering that the mind is unlimited, change whatever you want to make it exactly as you want. . . . . Very good.

You can stay in your room for as long as you want. You may want to stay a while longer or you may want to leave it now. Whenever you want to return to it, you'll be able to do so quickly and easily. Just close your eyes, get relaxed anyway you like, and just go to your very own room. The more often you go to it, the more quickly and easily it will happen. And when you want to leave it, you can leave anyway you want. It might be easiest just to walk out the door and return to your

usual state of consciousness. Or maybe you'll want a different way of leaving it. Makes no difference at all. However you leave it, you'll feel alert, fully functioning, very refreshed, and ready to go about your business.

The tape containing this script, like the tapes containing the other scripts in this interlude, is typically used only once or twice. After that, you'll have a way to go to your special place or meet your adviser (as discussed below) without needing a tape.

Your Inner Adviser or Guide

Many of us believe that there is some part of us that is wiser and more mature than the rest of the parts of our being. This part is variously called the strong part, the healthy part, the guide, or the inner adviser. Whatever the name, it's often believed that we'd be a lot better off if we paid more attention to this part and took its advice. This part is only an aspect of you, consisting of memories, experiences, and resources that may not be readily available to your everyday self. The inner-adviser technique is a way of getting in touch with this part and being able to discern its messages.

If you want to contact your inner adviser, you have to be open to surprises. Our guides aren't always what we expect. Its gender may not be the same as yours, it may be an animal rather than a person, it may communicate in ways you're not used to, and it may be a tough taskmaster instead of friendly and supportive as you expected. But that isn't surprising. Surely you've had the experience of an inner voice suggesting that you do something — change jobs, leave a lover, study, not eat the sundae — that the rest of you didn't agree with.

Psychologist Cory Hammond of the University of Utah relates a story that well illustrates how feisty some inner advisers can be. A client of his had an adviser who told her to read a certain book. The patient thought this was a stupid assignment and refused to do it. But she was then unable to contact her adviser. One time when she was trying to find him, another character appeared and said: "Look, you asked for his advice, and he told you what to do. If you didn't want his advice, you shouldn't have asked, and he's not coming back unless you follow through." The client then read the book and was surprised at how much she learned from it.

By now you may feel that this whole adviser business is a bit silly. How ridiculous to seek advice from some made-up character — especially if it's an old cat named Oscar — who gives suggestions you may not like. Many people feel like this at the start. But greater comfort soon sets in. It may help to know that some very famous people had what we would call inner guides. Mahatma Gandhi, for example, took a day off each week to listen to his "inner voice." People quickly get used to their guides. We know some people who consult them daily for advice and support on all kinds of issues. The only test of whether having a guide is worthwhile is if it serves your purposes. If you find you're doing better with it than without, then you know the answer.

The following script will help you find your guide. Use a tape on which you have first put your favorite relaxation instructions. As usual, feel free to change our words to better suit yourself.

Script 8: Your Inner Adviser or Guide

Time required: 5 to 7 minutes

As you sit here very relaxed and very much at peace, allow your mind to go to the place where you can meet your guide. Might be your special room, might be the beach, might even be someplace else. And as it does this, just be aware of any signs of life. . . . . Your adviser may have any kind of shape at all, might be a man or woman, might even be a squirrel or bird, might even look like a tree or flower. . . . . Doesn't make any difference at all what it looks like, just be aware of any living thing. . . . . Allow yourself some time to become aware of this living creature who is your guide. . . . . And if you feel you've given yourself enough time and no living thing appears, it's perfectly acceptable to make one up, to pretend that there's one there and it can be anything you want it to be. . . . .

When you imagine a living creature, make contact with it. Introduce yourself and find out its name. You'll probably find that it knows all about you, but it never hurts to be polite. When you want, tell your adviser why you want to have contact and what you'd like to get out of this meeting. . . . . You may have a question or two you want it to answer. . . . . You can stay with your guide as long as you want. . . . .

When you are ready to leave, establish a way of making contact in the future. Make sure you understand clearly where and how you can reach your guide, so that the two of you can continue working on whatever is in your interests. . . . . And when you've left your guide, you may want to continue relaxing for a while on your own, so that you can digest what just went on, or you may want to come back to everyday consciousness right away. In either case, when you are ready to come back to everyday reality, you can do so anyway you like, feeling refreshed, alert, and fully functioning, with the knowledge that

you have taken an important step toward accomplishing your goals.

Although we've discussed a room of your own and your inner adviser separately, there's really no need for the separation. Some people find that the best place to contact their inner adviser is in their room. Sometimes it even happens by accident there. One day June called to say that in her room, "I ran into someone — the strongest, wisest person I've ever met. She invited me to meet with her whenever I felt the need. All I have to do is to go to my room and call her." With the help of her adviser, June was able to resolve quickly several important issues in her life. If contacting your adviser in your room is appealing to you, you have only to go to your room and follow script 8.

An Outside Expert

The inner adviser is but one way of obtaining what might be called expert advice. There is also another way that many people have found quite beneficial. It involves getting advice not from an inner guide but from one or more advisers from the external world. Perhaps the best-known example of this technique is the experience of the highly successful businessman Napoleon Hill, related in his book *Think and Grow Rich.* He once wondered whom he would choose if he could somehow have a group of famous men as his personal and business advisers. He selected several famous historical figures he admired. Entirely on his own, he began talking to them while in trance. Every day for more than thirty years, Mr. Hill imagined himself going into a boardroom and meeting with his group of advisers.

He consulted them about whatever interested him and he found their advice invaluable.

There may be a person (or even a group of people) whose advice you would like to have: it might be a historical figure, a former therapist or coach or teacher, even a movie star. If you've ever thought, "I wonder how my coach [or sister, or Lee Iacocca, or anyone else] would handle this," then that's the person we have in mind. You can even use several different people for different situations: perhaps Ann Landers for personal issues, and Thomas Watson, Sr., or Lee Iacocca for business matters.

Guides and advisers can also be helpful to those whose main goal is learning more about themselves. Your inner guide is of course just the person to help you with this. You can also have another kind of help. Dr. Freud himself is available to your imagination, as is Dr. Jung, Dr. Rogers, Dr. Ellis, or any other therapists you admire. Or, if you have a different kind of expert in mind — such as Buddha, Jesus, or a Zen master — they are in your mind as well and available for consultation.

Before actually doing the exercise, you need to determine whom you want for your adviser. If you already know, you can plunge right in and make your tape. If not, take your time finding out, perhaps over several days. Just ask yourself whom you'd like to be able to talk to about the problems you're working on. It's generally best if you know something about the person, either from direct experience, books, or the media. And remember that the person need not be now alive to be of help to you.

As already mentioned, you can have a number of advisers meeting together with you, or whom you see separately, or whom you consult with for different issues. But, for purposes of clarity, we proceed as if you have only one.

When you know who your adviser is, make a tape that

includes enough instructions to help you become deeply relaxed, followed by a statement something like this one, substituting the name of your choice where we use Walter Cronkite.

Script 9: Getting Expert Advice

Time required: 5 to 10 minutes

Now that you're very comfortable, do you know where you're going to meet Mr. Cronkite? At his home or office, in a park, or maybe at your place? .... Wherever, why not go there now and meet him? .... And what do you imagine he's wearing? Is he dressed up in a suit, as you remember him on television, or is he more casually dressed today? And is he smoking his pipe? ....

[*The business about what he's wearing and if he's smoking his pipe are intended as aids to help you imagine him more clearly; you should use similar prompts about your character. In any mental-training exercise, anytime you have trouble clearly seeing something in your mind's eye, use similar prompts to help you.*]

As you introduce yourself, you may want to mention how much you've admired him all these years and how much you've wanted to talk to him about your career in television news; or maybe you want to tell him something else. .... Be sure to tell him, as specifically as you can, the kinds of things you want his help with and ask if he's willing. .... And now, since you're both there, you may want to give him more information about you, or maybe you want to jump in with a specific problem or issue you'd like his opinion on. .... Feel free to do whatever you want and to take as long as you want doing it. ....

When you want to leave, which may not be right now, be sure to make arrangements with Mr. Cronkite about meeting in the future. Be clear exactly how you can contact him. And when it's time to leave, do it anyway you like, coming back to the ordinary world remembering the salient points of your conversation with him, feeling invigorated and refreshed and fully alert, knowing you've gotten the best advice possible from the best person, and being ready to go on with your business.

Like the other tapes in this interlude, this one is typically used only once. When you want to meet your expert again, you'll know how to do it.

If you can dream it, you can do it.
                    — Walt Disney

CHAPTER 9

IMAGINING THE PROCESS

As we said in chapter 8, in result imagery you imagine having achieved the outcome you desire. In process imagery, on the other hand, you imagine yourself doing things in the way they need to be done so that you will realize your goals. Behavior therapists have given the name *mental rehearsal* to this kind of imagery; you rehearse in your mind things you want to do in reality.

Process imagery has received lots of publicity in recent years from athletes, many of whom use the terms *mind-scripting, visualizing,* and just plain *imagery* to describe it. Here, for example, is Olympic gold medal winner Mary Lou Retton, writing in the third person of her experience the night before she won her medal: "Before she dropped off to sleep inside the Olympic Village, Mary Lou did what she always did before a major competition — mindscripted it completely. She mentally ran through each routine, every move, imagining everything done perfectly." In the last chapter, we cited the example of Jack Nicklaus, who, before every shot, imagines himself hitting the ball in such a way that it will end up where he wants it. The great Boston Celtics basketball player and later coach Bill Russell has written about sitting with his eyes closed, "watching plays in my head. I was in my own private basketball laboratory, making mental blueprints for myself."

Another example comes from Chinese pianist Liu Chi Kung, who was imprisoned for seven years without access to a piano during the Cultural Revolution in China. Soon after his release he went on tour and critics were surprised that his playing was better than ever. When asked how this was possible, given that he hadn't practiced in seven years, he answered: "I did practice, every day. I rehearsed every piece I had ever played, note by note, in my mind."

In his study of high-achievers in American business, Charles Garfield notes that without even knowing there's a label for what they do, these men and women do a lot of mental rehearsal. He writes that "peak performers develop powerful mental images of the behavior that will lead to the desired results. They see in their mind's eye the result they want, and the actions leading to it. They rehearse. . . . They visualize, not as a substitute for thorough preparation and hard work but as an indispensable adjunct."

If you imagine yourself doing something in a particular way often enough, you will tend to do that thing in the way you imagine it. Imagine yourself behaving thus and such in a certain situation often enough, and you'll tend to behave that way. Imagine yourself feeling in such and such a way often enough, and you'll tend to feel that way, as the example of Harold in interlude 1 demonstrates. He imagined himself being calm and focused in his office, and that's exactly how he ended up feeling and being.

When you imagine yourself doing something in certain ways, the mind tends to take this as a real experience. Experiments here and in the Soviet Union have demonstrated that the appropriate muscles are activated when you imagine them performing some activity. When a skier imagines herself going down the slopes, her body will tend to make the movements she's imagining. When a boxer imagines himself throwing a punch, his arm and shoulder muscles will tense and often move. These people aren't trying to tense muscles or move. They're simply "doing their imagery," but in reaction to it the mind moves the muscles in appropriate ways, as if it actually were doing or getting ready to do what is being imagined. You really can program yourself to act and feel in certain ways, or, as Bill Russell put it, make mental blueprints for yourself.

We've often noticed the power of the mind when we guide clients in their imagery. Recently, for example, we were working with Andrea, who wanted help in preparing to talk to her boss about the unfair treatment she had been getting on the job. She'd been dreading the meeting, fearful that he would perceive her as just another whining woman unable to make it in the business world. After she was relaxed, we asked her to imagine the meeting. She immediately tightened up into a defensive crouch, as if expecting the worst, which she was. We then helped her relax again, asked her to feel the justice of her complaints, which were indeed justified, and then to imagine herself going into her boss's office feeling strong, entirely justified in what she was going to say, confident, and relaxed. Her posture quickly changed. She sat more upright and looked stronger and more confident.

The most important thing to remember when using process imagery is to imagine the act, feeling, or situation as you want it to be, not as you fear it might be. Imagining it as you're afraid it will be is just another example of negative self-hypnosis and you've probably already done too much of that. We want you to imagine it happening exactly the way you want it to happen.

Dan, a writer with a large advertising agency, is a good example of the effective use of process imagery. Although he writes good copy and has lots of creative ideas, he's always afraid of failing and of being fired, and these fears sometimes are so great as to make him totally unable to work or to make it very difficult to do the effective work he's capable of. He's not greatly ambitious; he only wants to feel more comfortable and confident in his work. He's quite willing to leave the winning of prizes to others in his agency.

One of Dan's problems was similar to one of Harold's: trying to do too much at once. And Dan had to learn the same thing Harold did: to work on only one thing at a time. Dan's desk was usually cluttered with work representing several different ads or campaigns. We got him to make folders for the different projects and have only one on his desk at a time. Then we had him imagine sitting at his desk, taking out one folder and opening it, looking through the material, and going to work on it and it alone. If an idea came for another ad, we had him imagine making a quick note about it before immediately turning back to the job at hand. We realize how simpleminded this whole procedure sounds, but it wasn't easy for Dan, who had rarely in his life concentrated on just one thing. The more he imagined focusing on one project at a time, the more he actually did it, and the results were similar to Harold's.

Another problem for Dan was that although he often had good ideas, he rarely voiced them in meetings with his creative director or other colleagues because of a fear of sounding stupid. He had been using negative self-hypnosis to his detriment for years, repeatedly playing variations of the same scene in his mind: he would voice an idea and everyone would say, "Jesus, is that dumb!" Because of his silence, some of his co-workers thought he didn't have any ideas and sometimes Dan was chagrined because an idea he didn't express was later voiced by someone else and accepted. Even at the cost of looking stupid, he wanted to express more of his ideas.

Once he was in a relaxed state, we had him repeatedly imagine speaking up when something occurred to him. The typical format was as follows:

> Now that you're relaxed, imagine feeling just as relaxed in a meeting with your creative director discussing ideas for the [name of product] ad. Allow an idea for it to come to your mind and nod your head when you have it. . . . . Good. Now imagine yourself immediately expressing your idea, feeling strong, positive, and confident as you do, knowing it is absolutely right and in your interests to express your idea. . . . . Very good. Imagine how proud you are now that you've said what's on your mind. . . . . Now allow another idea to surface and imagine yourself immediately expressing it, feeling confident, strong, and relaxed. You know you have good ideas. Isn't it nice to share them with others? . . . . Terrific. Now let's take a few moments and repeat the same process over and over, imagining yourself expressing your ideas to your creative director as soon as they occur to you, always feeling good about doing it, strong, proud, confident, positive, and relaxed. . . . . You're doing great.

As Dan got more comfortable with this, we gradually added more people to his imaginary meetings — another writer, another creative director, even the head of the agency. What we did in our office was merely preparation for the imagery work he did every day at work and at home. Within a few weeks, he was speaking up more often and even feeling good about it. Several colleagues recognized the change in him and expressed their approval, which made him feel even better.

But of course not all of Dan's ideas, or anyone else's, are good or useful, and we wanted to prepare him for the time when something he said would be bluntly rejected or laughed at. We told him he had to prepare for what he most feared. He said he was ready. We went over a list of acceptable responses to the negative reaction to his idea. Using the same format as above, we added the following sort of imagery after he expressed an idea:

> Imagine you throw out your idea and [someone else in the meeting] says, "Boy, that's pretty stupid" [or "That's dumb" or "That will never do" or "That doesn't work at all"]. Imagine that hearing those words stings, but not as much as you feared. You still feel good and strong and confident, knowing you're okay and re-alizing how proud you are of expressing yourself. You know that you're good, you know your ideas are worth consideration. . . . . Now imagine yourself replying, "Just thought I'd throw that out to see if you're awake," feeling good and confident and very proud that you're handling this situation so well. . . . .

At other times, we had him imagine responding with some-thing like, "Yeh, come to think of it, that doesn't really do it," feeling especially proud of himself because he could admit publicly that his idea wasn't a good one, still knowing that most of his ideas were good and useful. Dan practiced a number of different responses — everything from de-fending his idea to laughing at it — several times every day.

There are times when imagining the entire process is not necessary. A sprinter, for example, may well imagine every step of the race, but it's much more difficult for a marathon runner and also unnecessary. If you're going to give a twenty-minute presentation, you may want to imagine yourself saying every word the way you want to say it. But for a two-hour talk, that's a lot of work.

How do you handle such a situation? Simple. Pick out the salient points and imagine presenting them in the best way possible. For example, a person giving a two-hour talk may decide that the most important parts are the beginning (you've got to hook the audience), a part in the middle that is highly technical and difficult to understand (you have to present it well or you can put the audience to sleep), and the ending (you want to send everyone off with good feelings about you, the subject discussed, and themselves). So the speaker would imagine in detail only these parts.

How do you know which parts to choose to imagine in detail? There are only two criteria: choose those parts that are most important and those that give you the most difficulty.

Charles, a scientist, came to us for help because he wasn't accomplishing as much as he wanted. He had lots of good ideas, but carrying them out was more difficult than it used to be. The main problem was that he couldn't say no to all the requests that were being made of him, a problem that had grown increasingly worse as he became better known. Colleagues from all over the world called to get his advice on this and that point and to ask him to look over and comment on their manuscripts and research applications. Graduate students flocked to him for advice and assistance. More and more people asked him to serve on committees, give talks, and teach courses. He said yes to everyone and was losing himself in the process.

His problem is usually called lack of assertiveness, a very common problem for many people at their jobs or with their spouses, children, or relatives. Although Charles was flattered by the attention, his main desire was to be left alone to do his work. He recalled with tears how happy he had been years before when he wasn't getting much attention and could devote himself full-time to his research. He now wanted to reject most of the requests but didn't quite know how to do it and felt guilty at the prospect.

In order to deal with the guilt, we asked him to make a list of what he felt he absolutely had to do for his colleagues and students, the university, and his community. Charles compiled a very reasonable list. We agreed with him that what was on it clearly met his responsibilities as a professor, scientist, and citizen. But he was doing far more than what was on the list. So we asked him, "Are you agreeing that this much you will do, and no more?" His reply was, "That's what I want, but I need help."

Indeed he did. He had never been very assertive in any area of his life except for explicating and defending his own research. It was always easier to go along with the requests and suggestions of others than to risk antagonizing them or risk feeling guilty about rebuffing them. It would have taken years to go over every situation in which he had had trouble saying no, but that wasn't necessary. All the situations had the same pattern: someone would ask him to do something he didn't want to do or didn't have time to do and he would meekly agree. He had the greatest problem with women colleagues and students because he thought they were badly treated in his field and that someone should be supportive of them.

Charles was so timid that he couldn't even imagine being assertive with men in relatively easy situations. Turning to a technique we've mentioned before, we asked if he knew of anyone in his field who acted the way he wanted to. After thinking for a moment, he mentioned a former professor of his, long since dead. "I really admired the way Stan handled himself. He wasn't cruel, but he knew exactly what he wanted to do and he protected himself against anyone who might get in his way. I don't think he ever did anything he didn't want to do." That was all we needed. Stan would be Charles's model in fantasy and in life.

We taught Charles to relax and had him draw up a list of situations that were difficult to handle. Starting with the easier ones, we worked our way through the list. Here is an excerpt from one session:

As you sit there feeling comfortably relaxed, imagine that you're in your office and the phone rings. You pick it up and say hello. Imagine that the caller is Dr. Smith from Brussels, and imagine that you exchange some chitchat and then he asks if you have time to review a research grant proposal he is preparing. . . . . Good. Now you know that although you're interested in his research, you don't have the time to review his proposal. It's in your interest to say no. But maybe you aren't yet ready to do that. So imagine Stan replying to the request, feeling confident that he's doing the right thing. Always so confident and relaxed, so strong. Imagine exactly, word for word, what Stan would say. . . . . Fine, that's good. And imagine how strong Stan must feel, knowing he's doing what's best for him. Allow yourself to feel what Stan feels — confidence, strength, certainty of purpose, comfort with himself. . . . . Doesn't that feel good? Just as Stan felt that good, so can you. Just as Stan protected his time for research, so can you.

In a moment let's go through that scene again. But this time let's see if you can say some of Stan's words. Not all of them, but at least a few of them. In your mind you can switch back and forth between you and Stan. Imagine you're in the office and the phone rings. You say hello and it's Dr. Smith asking if you can review his grant proposal. You know you don't have time to do it and you feel good knowing that about yourself. Now imagine yourself and Stan feeling strong and sure, very comfortable and confident, telling Dr. Smith you're sorry, but you're absolutely swamped. You and Stan, strong and sure, relaxed and confident, saying you're really sorry, but you simply can't do it. . . . . And notice how good it feels to be honest and to protect yourself. . . . . Very good. And now, just as Stan would, change the topic. Ask Dr. Smith if you'll see him at the meeting in Toronto in November. . . . . Very nice. You should practice this scene in your mind as often as you can after getting relaxed, at least several times a day. The more you practice it, the more you'll realize that just as Stan protected his time, so can you. Just as Stan protected himself and felt very good about it, so can you.

Using Stan as a model worked beautifully. Whenever there was a problem — and there were many — we turned to Stan. One time Charles was despondent because he was in the middle of an important experiment and an all-day meeting that he had long ago agreed to attend was coming up in a few days. We asked if he couldn't just skip it, but he was horrified by the thought. So we asked how Stan would handle it.

"I know exactly what he'd do," said Charles. "He was a great showman. He would go early to the meeting, say hello to everyone and then announce that much to his sorrow, he was in the middle of an important experiment and couldn't stay. He'd apologize so profusely that most people there would feel appreciative that he'd left his experiment long enough to come say hello. Some would even feel guilty for having taken him away from his valuable work. By then Stan would be back in his laboratory."

We had Charles visualize Stan handling the situation in

this way and then, as per the example above, had him say Stan's lines as much as he could, with the suggestion that he feel strong, relaxed, and very confident as he did so. We told him to practice this as often as possible at home, although we weren't sure what would happen, since the meeting was only a few days off. Charles was aglow when he came to the next session a week later. Although he would never have Stan's flair for showmanship, he had done pretty much what he thought Stan would have done. He was deservedly very pleased with himself.

The last big hurdle was women. Because of his perception that women in the sciences were mistreated, Charles found it very difficult to turn down their requests. But he had to. Increasing numbers of his colleagues and students were women and he had to find a way to deal with them. We kept reminding him that he had made plenty of provision to help women in his list of obligations and that he had promised himself "this much and no more." We used the same basic imagery format as before, again calling up the image of Stan whenever needed.

A typical imagery session dealing with women went as follows:

Now that you're relaxed, imagine yourself in your laboratory checking on the equipment, when that bright new student, Jane, comes up and asks if you can help with her experiment. Imagine the feelings you would have. You like her and want to help, but you also know that you don't have the time and that she has her own adviser to turn to. You realize that it is in your best interest to tell her you're sorry, but you're too busy. . . . . Good. Now imagine what Stan would tell her. He would say that while he'd love to help her out, he's so swamped by work that it's simply impossible. Now imagine you or Stan telling her that, in a voice that's clear, firm, strong, yet friendly. Word by word, telling her what you need to tell her, what you need to do for yourself, for the good of your work. . . . . You're doing very well. How was that? [Charles says it went fine, so we up the ante.]

Stay with that image and continue to feel good and relaxed. Imagine that Jane looks very disappointed and says that she was really counting on you because she's not getting along with her adviser. If you don't help her, she doesn't know where she will turn. . . . . Imagine how you would feel. You would be touched. You would want to rescue her. . . . . At the same time, a voice in your mind says: "This much and no more. You have your own work to do." The message is repeated over and over, and each time the voice gets louder and more insistent until it's shouting: *"This much and no more. You have your own work to do and you have to take care of yourself."* Hear that voice; hear it and heed it. . . . . Feel your strength and your resolve growing; imagine yourself strong, powerful, confident, resolute. Imagine yourself saying to Jane in a strong, relaxed, and friendly manner: "I'd very much like to help you, but if I do I'm going to do damage to my own work. I'm truly sorry to have to say no. But if it's any solace, I like your ideas and I think we might be able to work together someday. If you're interested in a year or two, let me know. . . . ."

Imagine how good you feel and how proud, being honest and being true to yourself and still offering Jane something to look forward to. . . . . Splendid. Now this imagery is something you should practice as often as you can, growing more confident, more relaxed, more resolved each time you go through it in your mind, more and more relaxed, more and more confident, more and more resolved until it won't even be an issue anymore, just an expression of the way you are, protecting yourself as Stan did, taking care of yourself as Stan did, and doing what's best for you.

We worked with Charles for sixteen sessions over five months. By the end of that time, he was far more assertive than ever before in his life and he had what he wanted: the freedom to pursue his work without constant interruptions. He still sometimes felt guilty but usually not for long. That voice in his head kept asserting itself: "*This much and no more. You have your own work to do and you have to take care of yourself.*" Colleagues and students noticed the change in him and reacted accordingly. He was no longer known as the guy who was always available for anything. Fewer people felt free to interrupt him or make requests, and that suited him just fine.

We ran into Charles not long ago, several years after our work with him had ended, and he said his life continues to go well. He no longer uses the imagery every day, but does one or two sessions a week to keep in practice. When a difficult situation is in the offing, he does more sessions to get himself ready to cope with it.

Before doing the basic process imagery exercise below (script 10), make a list of what processes you want to imagine. Take as much time as you need, in as many sessions as you need, to make a list of the behaviors you want to rehearse. These are the things you have to do to achieve your goals. We've already given a number of examples, but here a few more: eating only a salad for lunch; saying no to pressure from Fred to have a drink; sitting down and studying from 6 P.M. to 10 P.M.; telling your boss about your idea and pushing it if he or she is reluctant; calling up that certain someone and asking for a date or saying you'd like to talk to see if the two of you can straighten out your differences; telling your spouse that it's crucial the two of you have a serious talk about the trouble you're having with Johnny. Remember that the behaviors have to be specific; otherwise, you won't be able to imagine them. The idea is to do something in a certain way, in a particular situation, and perhaps with certain other people.

When you have your list, put it away for a day or two and then come back to it, making any changes you want. Then arrange the items on the list from easiest to most difficult. As usual, start with the easiest items.

Make a tape that includes brief relaxation instructions — you shouldn't need much to get you relaxed by this point — followed by a minute or so of suggestions to imagine yourself having achieved your goal. Then give instructions such as the ones in the following script to structure your process imagery. As per our example, deal with only one process, event, or experience. In other words, don't try to do too much. And be sure to allow enough time and provide enough detail for you to get very involved in the behavior you're imagining. If you have trouble imagining yourself doing what you want to do, either try something easier or imagine someone else with whom you can identify doing it. If you do the latter, be sure to include instructions (as in our example of Charles and Stan and as in interlude 3) that allow you to step into your model's shoes and assume his or her role.

Starting difficult conversations, whether with an employer, spouse, child, or someone else, is a frightening task for many people. Script 10 is part of one we used with Andrea, the woman who wanted to talk to her boss, Fred, about how she was being treated on the job. You'll have to modify it to suit your needs. Since her biggest stumbling block was her opening lines, that's what we focus on here. Note that we start by recalling a past success and use a number of posthypnotic suggestions (the subject we discuss in chapter 11). We also use lots of repetition, just as you should.

Script 10: Mental Rehearsal or Process Imagery

Time required: 5 to 12 minutes

Now that you're pleasantly relaxed, recall the time you complained to your neighbor about playing the stereo so loud in the middle of the night. Get that experience clearly in your mind. Remember how determined, resolved, and fully in control you felt as you walked downstairs to his apartment. . . . . How those feelings increased as you knocked on his door, said hello, and then made your request for more quiet. . . . . Recall how proud you felt even before he had a chance to respond. . . . . And remember how well it worked out and how wonderful you felt about your accomplishment. . . . . That's right, very good. You can feel those feelings again. Just as strong, just as determined, just as much in control, just as proud and wonderful. Just as you handled that situation magnificently, you can handle other situations magnificently. Just as you felt wonderful about yourself then, you can feel wonderful about talking to your boss.

Hang on to those feelings of strength, power, pride. Hang on to them as we continue.

Now imagine yourself walking into Fred's office, feeling as calm and confident as you feel right now, feeling as strong and justified about the request you're going to make as you feel right now — as you did when you walked to your neighbor's. . . . . Just as you're feeling your comfort and strength and confidence right now, so you can feel it in your walk and the way you hold yourself on your way to his office. You know full well that your complaints are totally justified and that you have every right to demand better treatment.

Feel your resolve, your strength, as you enter his office. It shows in your face, in your walk, in the way you sit down, in the way you say hello to Fred. Imagine this as clearly as possible. . . . . Very good.

Now imagine Fred greeting you, saying his usual "Good to see you. How are the kids?" . . . . Imagine yourself answering and inquiring about his family, still feeling strong, calm, and determined to make your complaint as soon as the chitchat is over. . . . . Strong and relaxed, just as you were in your neighbor's apartment . . . . feeling really good. Now imagine there's a break in the conversation and you, feeling very good about yourself, very strong, say: "Fred, I need to talk to you about something." Imagine the confidence and relaxation in your voice, reflecting the strength of your resolve. Hear your words sounding firm, strong, persuasive. . . . .

Imagine yourself continuing: "I feel like I'm treated unfairly because I'm a woman," and as you say the words, feel the strength and the resolve in your voice — firm, powerful, yet fully in control, very calm. . . . . That's very good. And imagine how proud you are of yourself. . . . .

That's terrific. Now do it again, just the parts about feeling strong and calm as you walk down the hall into his office, carrying yourself erect and proud, feeling the same way, and then the chatting, keeping your calm and resolve, and then your opening lines. . . . . That's right, firm, resolved, fully in control, imagine the whole scene, always feeling confident and strong. . . . . And then so proud of yourself, feeling so good about yourself. . . . . A very strong, very determined woman.

Just as you tapped into inner sources of strength, control, resolve, and deep calm years ago with your neighbor, you can tap into those same resources when you talk to Fred. Just as you felt so strong and confident and calm then, you can feel the same when you talk to Fred. Just as you felt proud and reached your goal with your neighbor, so you can feel proud and achieve your goal with Fred. Strong and relaxed, firm and confident, very much in control. As it was then, so it will be

when you talk to Fred. Just as you triumphed then, you can triumph now.

You should listen to this tape and imagine this behavior every day, several times a day. And each time, you'll feel more comfortable, more relaxed, more confident of your ability to carry it out, to talk to Fred about your complaints. More and more comfort each time, greater strength and resolve. Know that as you tapped into inner resources in the past, you will do so again with Fred.

And when you're ready, allow your eyes to open, wiggle around a little to orient yourself, and be fully alert, fully functioning, feeling very good about yourself, very strong, very proud.

Since most people will have a number of processes they'll want to imagine, you can make several tapes at the same time, following the same format on each — relaxation first, then a brief imaging of having accomplished your goal, followed by detailed suggestions for imagining one of your behaviors, a different behavior on each tape.

Listen to the tape with the easiest process to imagine at least twice a day for a week or so, until you are very comfortable imagining yourself carrying out that behavior in reality. Then you can move on to the next scene.

If you don't get more comfortable with the scene after one or two attempts, or if it's very hard to imagine in the first place, you're trying to do something that's too difficult. Move this item down in your list and start with something easier. Another option is to use a hero or model (as Charles did with Stan) until you get more comfortable. Still another option is to use a memory of a past success at or near the beginning of the tape, as we did with Andrea, to strengthen yourself.

Symbolic Imagery

After listening to script 10 a few times, Andrea came up with an image that summarized her feelings of strength and resolution and also suggested "getting a grip on things": a huge, heavily muscled hand tightly grasping a large bag. This image had a powerful effect on her and she used it several times a day along with the imagery of talking to Fred. Four days after starting with this image, she had her talk with him and it went even better than anticipated.

You should always feel free to make use of symbolic imagery in your mental training. If wilted lettuce suggests relaxation to you, then imagine the lettuce when you want to relax. If a fist suggests strength, then imagine a fist when you want to feel stronger. If a cool washcloth on your head suggests calm and healing (and an end to a headache), then imagine the washcloth. Symbolic images work much the same as cue words and phrases, quickly evoking the desired feelings (after some practice, of course).

Summary: Guidelines for Imagining the Means

• Make a list of the scenes, behaviors, or feelings you want to rehearse and arrange the items on it in ascending order from the least to the most difficult. Make sure that what you rehearse is the way you want things to be, not the way they've been or the way you fear they will be.

• Make a tape of relaxation directions — they should be very brief by now — followed by suggestions to imagine having achieved your goal (this, too, should be brief), and then record process imagery in *great detail* of the easiest scene on your list. If you have trouble imagining yourself doing the item, imagine someone you admire doing it first, then include yourself as you're able to (for more information about this technique, see interlude 3).

As an alternative to the above format, use recollection of a past success instead of goal imagery. Another option, which will make for a longer tape, is to use them all: relaxation plus goal imagery plus recollection of a past success, then process imagery.

• Remember to put a lot of positive comments in the tape, things like "that's very good," "wonderful," "great," and "you're doing fine."

• Listen to this tape at least twice a day for a week or more until you are thoroughly comfortable with the imagery. Then go on to the next tape and scene. You can also practice the scene without listening to the tape anytime you have a spare moment.

• Don't neglect your goal imagery when doing mental rehearsal. If you're not including at least brief goal imagery in your process imagery tapes, at least once every other day get relaxed and spend a moment or two imaging one or more aspects of having reached your goal.

A MODEL OF YOUR OWN

In interlude 2 we presented the idea of an internal or external guide of your own, an imaginary figure whose advice and support you can count on. A model is similar in some ways but differs in one important respect, and it has been helpful to so many successful people that we offer it separately.

Whereas guides offer suggestions for what you can do, models show you. They are people you want to emulate in certain respects: you want to project the poise and power of Martin Luther King, Jr., in addressing a group, to feel the unflappability of Chris Evert Lloyd in starting a game, to project the nonchalance of Humphrey Bogart in talking to women, and so on. There's no need for your models to be famous. Many of the best models are relatives, friends, or co-workers who handle certain situations in ways you'd like to.

Models are especially useful when you are barely able even to imagine yourself doing something you want to do or when you don't do as good a job of it as someone else.

Basketball great Bill Russell used this method to learn new moves.

> I was working on learning how to take an offensive rebound and move quickly to the hoop. It's a fairly simple play . . . but I didn't execute it well and [Eural] McKelvey did. Since I had an accurate version of his technique in my head I started playing with the image, running back the picture several times and each time inserting a part of me for McKelvey. Finally I saw myself making the whole move, and I ran this over and over, too. When I went into the game I grabbed an offensive rebound and put it in the basket just the way McKelvey did. It seemed natural, almost as if I were just stepping into the film.

Guides and models need not be separate. Some people find that they can combine the two roles into one imaginary figure, as shown in this example:

Ralph, a very successful financier, very shy and very formal in manner, had stayed away from women almost all of his life but now, close to fifty, decided he wanted to get married. This goal made sense for him, but the problem was that he could barely talk to a woman outside of a business setting without breaking out in a sweat.

Our work with Ralph consisted of a number of methods, but the model imagery was essential. His hero in the how-to-relate-to-women department was Cary Grant, who Ralph thought had just the right combination of assertiveness, confidence, and sensitivity. Although Ralph could not at first imagine introducing himself to a strange woman and having a relaxed, confident conversation, or even having this kind of conversation with a woman he'd already been introduced to, he could easily imagine Cary Grant doing that. So we had him imagine this many times, gradually imagining himself in the role of Mr. Grant (as Ralph referred to him). Ralph did this repeatedly until he could comfortably imagine himself talking to different women.

Meanwhile, we had Ralph discuss his problem with his hero, ask Mr. Grant's perspective on man–woman relationships, and obtain specific advice for himself. Whenever he wanted to speak to his hero, he needed only to say his cue phrase, "strong and calm," several times, followed by "Might we have a chat, Mr. Grant?" It was all very formal at the beginning.

Our work took a number of months, which isn't surprising considering that Ralph had spent almost fifty years avoiding women. But gradually he became more comfortable meeting, talking to, and going out with women. To his surprise, he found that women liked him and sought his company. He began, under Mr. Grant's tutelage, to appreciate himself — his sensitivity, his independence, his superior problem-solving abilities, and his graciousness. One thing that we like about inner advisers and other imaginary experts is that people are usually far more willing to listen to them than they are to us. We had told Ralph about his good qualities many times, but he seemed unable to hear us. When Mr. Grant told him essentially the same things, his hearing improved.

Whenever Ralph anticipated behaving in a new way with a woman — for example, telling her he liked her, expressing physical affection, sharing personal thoughts and feelings — he first imagined the way Mr. Grant would do it and then saw himself doing what his hero had done.

Ralph made vast changes in his ability to deal with women. One day, he excitedly reported that his hero had suggested they drop the formality and use first names; and further, if Ralph agreed, Cary would just show up whenever he felt he was wanted without Ralph having to call him. That

Cary Grant now accepted him as a friend and equal, which is how Ralph interpreted the conversation, boosted his self-esteem and confidence even higher. He had made Cary Grant his own — which is as it should be, because the Cary Grant Ralph knew was only a stronger, more confident side of himself. Although Ralph will never be Cary Grant, he had found the Cary Grant side of himself, and that is what helped him achieve his goal.

Models are very powerful generators of personal change. If you want to use one, you first need to decide whom you want to emulate and in what *very specific* ways. Then you should make a tape that provides the instructions, which need to be very detailed. You should listen to that tape at least twice a day for at least a week. The more you listen to it, the better.

How can you go about making a script of the specific behaviors you want to imitate? We can do no better than quote Bill Russell, a true master of this art. As a high-school player, whenever he was on the bench he closely observed two of his teammates.

> Every time one of them would make one of the moves I liked, I'd close my eyes just afterward and try to see the play in my mind. In other words, I'd try to create an instant replay on the inside of my eyelids. Usually I'd catch only part of a particular move the first time I tried this; I'd miss the head work or the way the ball was carried or maybe the sequence of the steps. But the next time I saw the move I'd catch a little more of it, so that soon I could call up a complete picture of, say, Bill Treu's spinning right-handed lay-up from the left side of the basket.

Here are our suggestions from two sessions with a woman named Randi who wanted to be more "forward," as she put it, with men. Her model was an old friend, Molly, who was very confident and assertive with men and very popular with them. We are breaking one of our own rules — don't try to do too much in one tape — in presenting this script. We're doing this only to demonstrate what the larger picture looks like. In our work with Randi, the first tape consisted of only the first two paragraphs of script 11, about getting ready to go to a party, repeated a number of times. The next tape consisted of one rerun of those paragraphs followed by the entering-the-party scene, repeated a number of times. You should certainly break your work up in this fashion. Randi had prepared carefully for her sessions. She had closely observed Molly and could imagine very specifically the things we suggested to her. When we said, for instance, to recall how Molly walked, a wealth of detail came into her mind.

Script 11: A Model of Your Own

Time required: 5 to 9 minutes

Now that you're comfortably relaxed, imagine in your mind's eye Molly getting ready to go to a party. Imagine her anticipation, her confidence, and how these feelings show in the way she thinks about the party. What is she saying to herself? . . . . Now imagine the way she chooses her clothes and how she dresses. . . . . The way she puts on her makeup. . . . . Get into those feelings as much as you can. . . . . Fine, that's great.

Now let's do it again: Molly anticipating going to the party, the thoughts and feelings of anticipation, excitement, confidence, and joy she has as she chooses her clothes, dresses, puts on her makeup. And this time put yourself in her place part of the time. Feel some of her feelings, think some of her thoughts, act and be as she is. . . . . Sometimes it's her, sometimes you, sometimes who knows who. . . . . Feeling really good, really looking forward with enthusiasm to seeing who'll be there tonight. And it's perfectly fine if sometimes it's Molly with the feelings and sometimes you, and you might even get confused, not knowing which is Molly and which is you having these wonderful feelings of confidence, strength, and anticipation. . . . . You're doing fine.

Now let's follow Molly to the party. Imagine closely how she walks into the room: the look on her face . . . . the way her legs move . . . . the way she holds herself. . . . . All the things you've admired for so long. Really study her — the openness and anticipation showing on her face, in her eyes, her smile, the way she looks around. . . . . Her confidence and strength coming through in the way she holds herself, the way she moves, the way she walks. . . . . She's such a good model for you.

Now let's imagine your face looking like hers. It's still you and your face but you're projecting the look Molly does, and sometimes it's you and sometimes it's her, and it doesn't make any difference because the look and the feelings that come across are what count. . . . .

Now let yourself get another good look and feel for how she walks into the room, her legs and feet moving, her posture, the swing of her arms. . . . . Good. And now imagine yourself doing some of that, walking exactly like that, projecting an air of strength and confidence, yet open and receptive at the same time. . . . . Sometimes it's Molly, sometimes Randi, sometimes it's hard to tell who it is. It's you walking like Molly or maybe Molly walking like Molly or who knows who, but it's the attitude and feeling conveyed that's important. . . . . Very good. Once more, imagine Molly walking into the room, every detail of her look, her carriage, her movements, and the confidence and attraction conveyed by her. . . . . Great. And now it's you, walking and looking and moving and swinging your arms just like Molly. . . . . The same attitude of putting yourself out there, letting the world know you're interested and interesting, that you're someone worth noticing. . . . . As much like Molly as you can. . . . . You're doing really fine.

You should listen to this tape, Randi, at least twice a day.

The more you listen to it, the easier it will be to imagine the scenes in detail, with every little movement and gesture becoming clearer and clearer. The more you listen, the easier it will be for you to imagine yourself doing what Molly does, feeling as she does, and projecting the attitudes she does. The more you listen to this tape, and others we will make for you, the more confident you will feel, the more you will act and be with men the way Molly is, and the sooner you will get what you want.

Of course this was just the beginning of our work with Randi. We went on to deal with many other situations using the same method: for example, starting conversations with strangers, asking men for their phone numbers, asking them out, paying for meals with men, initiating physical and sexual intimacy, rejecting sexual advances, giving her feelings and opinions about many things. Molly was the model in each case.

In case you're concerned that Randi might have become a carbon copy of Molly, it didn't happen. Randi could no more become Molly than Ralph could become Cary Grant. It's paradoxical but true that by copying someone else both Randi and Ralph became more themselves. Though Randi's newfound assertive style started as a copy of Molly's, it was quickly branded by Randi's own personality. No one, including Molly, ever accused her of being a copy-cat, just as no one accused Bill Russell of trying to be Eural McKelvey or Bill Treu, though he made himself into a better Bill Russell by copying some of their moves.

One's life is dyed the color of his imagination.
                                    — Marcus Aurelius

CHAPTER 10

WHAT TO SAY WHEN
YOU TALK TO YOURSELF

We all talk to ourselves more or less continuously — not
the kind of talking that others are aware of, but the quiet
kind that goes on only inside our heads. As long as you're
alive, your brain is always active and a lot of what it does
is talk to itself, mainly about you. Unfortunately, most people give themselves a hard time, perhaps because critical
parents, teachers, and others have led them to believe mainly
negative things about themselves. Their self-messages come
down to all the things that are wrong with them. They tell
themselves "I'm bad," I'm just too selfish," "I sound like a
complete fool," "I always manage to say the wrong thing,"
"I'll never make it to the top," "I fail at everything I do,"
"Why bother, I can't do anything right," and other such
self-defeating things. And it gets even worse. We have had
clients whose main message to themselves was "You're an
idiot," "You're an asshole," "You're a total incompetent,"
and similar statements.

   If what we're saying sounds strange to you or if you
want to do an experiment that often has fascinating results,

try the following. Carry a small notebook in your pocket or purse and jot down all instances of negative self-talk as soon as possible. Do this conscientiously for a week or two and you'll have a pretty good idea of what you're doing to yourself. We should mention, however, that some very self-deprecating people carry their notebooks around for weeks and write nothing in them. They are so used to the negative statements they make to themselves that they aren't aware there's anything negative or unusual in them.

One of the most self-critical men we've ever met fit into this category. He told us that he hadn't noticed any negative statements in the previous week and then proceeded to make more than a dozen of them in the next thirty minutes. When we tried to call his attention to some of them, his response was, "They're not negative statements, they're just reality." We say to you, as we said to him, that it's not reality and it's not natural to tell yourself that you're inadequate, that you're stupid, that you can't do anything right, that you're an idiot, that you don't deserve good things.

If you have trouble recognizing negative self-talk, remember that it consists of any and all statements that are critical of yourself — your abilities, assets, and prospects. "But wait a minute," you say. "It's true that some things are harder for me than for other people and that I don't have an unlimited number of skills and resources." We have no quarrel with that statement. We are not implying that everyone is a Benjamin Franklin, a Gloria Steinem, an Albert Einstein, a Maria Callas, or an Arnold Schwarzenegger. We all have areas of difficulty and limitations. It's reality to acknowledge you won't be as good a physicist as Einstein, but that doesn't justify self-statements such as "I'll never be good at physics." Very few of us will sing like Maria Callas, but that doesn't justify statements like "I can't carry a tune. I'll never be able to sing."

If your self-statements merely reflect reality, there's no problem, but make sure that that is indeed the case. Too many people's self-talk goes far beyond reality and that's the problem. They tell themselves they're stupid when in fact they're just not as bright as some incredible standard they've set for themselves. They tell themselves they can't sing when in fact they can, though perhaps not well enough to make a living at it. They tell themselves they look like hell when in fact they have pleasing builds, though not like Jane Fonda's.

Here is what Liz, a computer programmer who at first couldn't believe she went around saying negative things to herself, wrote in her notebook one morning:

Tues.
- I'll never understand Ada [a computer language used at her job].
- I'm not as smart as the other programmers.
- I should have settled for nursing.
- It takes forever for me to learn anything new.
- I'm a living example of Murphy's Law. If there's a wrong way to do something, that's how I'll do it.
- They'll fire me if they see how stupid I am.
- I'm just a dumb shit.

These thoughts were repeated throughout the day with small variations, but enough is enough. After reading the messages she had written down over a week, she had a clearer picture than ever before of how she suffocated herself. No wonder she had trouble learning. Her attention was not on the computer language but on what a dumb, terrible person she was.

Negative self-talk will usually result in negative emotions and unfortunate results. Self-fulfilling prophecies are quite common. We start believing our own propaganda and bring about what we fear. "If I don't get a promotion, I'll get more and more upset and end up with a migraine." Indeed you will! "If Joan won't marry me, it'll be a catastrophe." It sure will if you think that way.

Happily, the converse is also true. Positive self-talk will generate good feelings and will facilitate adaptive reactions. Success rather than failure is likely to go with the person who says, "There's no point in getting all upset. I will take it easy, step by step, and I'll probably do just fine." It would be best of all if we were naturally nice to ourselves and sent mainly positive messages. But very often that's not the case. Second-best is to learn to replace self-downing and self-critical ideas with self-accepting and self-affirming cognitions.

It's at this point that we sometimes get a complaint from clients or audiences. "You want me to repeat nice things to myself, but that's artificial and just simpleminded positive thinking. Besides, it doesn't work." Our response is that there's nothing artificial about talking to yourself. It's a natural human tendency. We seek only to modify it to make it more positive, more constructive. Surely you would not want to argue that saying only negative things to yourself is natural. Are the messages we send to ourselves simpleminded? They certainly are in a sense, all coming down to either "You're a bad, incompetent person" or "You're a good, competent person." Simpleminded the messages may be, but they are extremely powerful.

Does it help to change what you say to yourself? It most certainly does. One of the most effective psychotherapies now available, cognitive behavior therapy, is largely based on changing behavior by changing what people tell themselves and how they view themselves. Tell yourself often enough that you'll fail and you almost certainly will, and you'll just as certainly feel bad about yourself. Tell yourself often enough that you'll succeed and you dramatically improve your chances of succeeding and of feeling good.

One way of using positive self-talk that we've illustrated a number of times in previous chapters is to include positive statements in your imagery work. Tell yourself things like the following (the words in italics represent shortened versions that can be used at any time):

- "I know my material and I've done my homework. I'm sure *I'll give a good talk.*"
- "*I'm interesting, attractive, and lots of fun.* I deserve to meet a nice woman [or man]."
- "I've handled difficult situations before and usually done well. *I can also do well this time.*"
- "I really deserve the promotion, yet I know there's a chance I won't get it. If I don't, I'll be hurt and disappointed, but *I'll get over it.*"
- "I'll stay calm. . . . I'll be just fine. . . . If I start feeling tense, I'll remember to relax and breathe slowly and deeply for a few moments . . . and *I'll be just fine.*"
- "Just as I pulled things together in the X deal [a similarly difficult case in the past], *I'll pull them together here.*"
- [For use in a situation where you didn't do well] "I really made a bad impression and there's not much I can do about it now. That's really not me, that's not how I usually come across. *Next time I'll prepare more and come across as I usually do.*"

You might want to go over some of the imagery examples in previous chapters now and see how we've used similar positive suggestions in them. You should always incorporate such statements into your imagery, whether the longer kinds of imagery you do with a tape or the shorter kinds you do whenever you have a spare moment to relax and imagine accomplishing one of your goals. Our examples also include positive self-talk in a more general way — focusing on things you can do and will be able to do, and focusing on positive, strong emotions.

Remind yourself of past successes, of times you've done well, of times you've overcome obstacles, of times you've felt good. Just as you felt good then, you can feel good now. Just as you overcame adversity then, you can overcome adversity now. Just as you succeeded in X, you can succeed in Y.

When considering positive self-talk, many people get caught up in past failures, saying things like "Well, that sounds great, but the fact is I've never been good at math," or "I don't see how I can focus on successes when it's a fact that I really blew it at the last interview." We're sure you're right. If you're human, you've failed many times. But that's no reason to focus on those events or to let them destroy your chances for success in the future.

In John Steinbeck's version of the King Arthur story, there's a comment about failure that we often read to people we work with. After the young Arthur is bested in a fight, he does what many people do — goes on at great length about what a klutz and failure he is. Merlin, a very wise consultant, tires of it and tells Arthur the following: "Somewhere in the world there is defeat for everyone. Some are destroyed by defeat, and some made small and mean by victory. Greatness lives in one who triumphs equally over defeat and victory." Arthur learns his lesson and goes on to claim Excalibur.

This lesson is not merely a child's story. In their highly regarded study of successful leaders in American industry and public life, Warren Bennis and Burt Nanus conclude that "the most impressive and memorable quality of the leaders we studied was the way they responded to failure. They simply don't think about failure, don't even use the word, relying on such synonyms as 'mistake,' 'glitch,' 'bungle.' . . . One of them said during the course of an interview that 'a mistake is just another way of doing things.' " Which brings to mind the story of Thomas Edison, who, after another unsuccessful attempt to make a workable light bulb, was asked if he had failed again. His response: "I didn't fail. I just discovered another way not to invent the light bulb."

It's probably true that the most successful people have failed more times than others simply because they've tried more things. Abraham Lincoln, though rightly considered as one of our greatest successes, also had a lot of experience with failure. He twice failed in business and lost seven elections for various offices. Other people might have told themselves they just weren't cut out for business or elective office, but Lincoln kept on believing in himself and what he wanted to do. Successful people don't focus on their failures because there's no point in doing so. Focusing on and reminding yourself of failures will only produce more failures. Learn what you can from failures and then let go of them, focusing only on past successes and what needs to be done next.

If that last suggestion seems too difficult to accomplish, do something about it. Create a process imagery exercise in which you imagine yourself acknowledging that you didn't do as well as you liked, saying that's too bad, and then telling yourself you'll prepare better and do better the next time. Before ending the session, remind yourself of a past success. This is a good place to use your skills at restructuring imagery. After you've acknowledged your failure, reduce its intensity by stepping out of the image and seeing it separated (if you were merged with it), and then push it into the distance, making it smaller, dimmer, fuzzier, until it disappears or is barely discernible. When you imagine your past success or how well you'll handle a similar situation in the future, merge into it and make it colorful, clear, large, appropriately loud — altogether very strong and inviting. Do this exercise regularly for a week or two, using different kinds of failures and varying what you say to yourself, and you'll find it's easier to accept failure and go beyond it.

Cue words or phrases, discussed in chapter 6, are a kind of positive self-talk. Saying "calm and cool" to yourself is, after all, a suggestion that you will be just that. Any long statement that you make to yourself can be shortened into a slogan or cue phrase that you can use at any time, as indicated by our list on page 183. If you start out with, "I'm good at selling cars — I was incredibly good with Mercedes — and deserve to get a good job," you can shorten it to something like "I'm a good salesman." As long as the shorthand carries the intended meaning to yourself, it will serve its function.

Let's go back to Liz, the computer programmer we mentioned earlier in this chapter. We helped her draw up counterstatements to the negative ones she was making. At first, the positive statements were used to argue with the negative ones; in the long run, the positive ones were supposed to replace the negative ones. When Liz heard herself say "I'll never understand Ada," she was to immediately challenge the statement, something like this: "That's crap. I learned Fortran, Pascal, C, and a bunch of others. It feels hard right now, but I know I'll master Ada." As often as she remembered, at any time during the day, she was to repeat the last three words to herself: *I'll master Ada.* We also used some goal imagery with her in which she imagined that her life after using Ada was merely routine.

When she caught herself saying she was a dumb shit, we had her repeat a version of this: "That's ridiculous. I'm just upset and saying silly things because it's so hard with a new language. The fact is that I had the highest IQ in my high school and am one of the brightest people I've ever met. *I'm a very smart woman.*" The last sentence was the one she was to repeat as often as possible.

In a like way, we helped her draw up counterarguments for each of the rest of her negative self-statements. She was to use the counter each time she made the corresponding negative statement. There was a shorthand for each positive statement, shorter and easier comments she was to use as much as possible: *"I'm more than competent," "I'm good," "I do quite well,"* and *"I'm a very smart woman."*

As we hope our examples make clear, you need not just positive self-statements but ones that directly counter the negative ones you've been making. The more directly the positive statements address the criticisms, doubts, and complaints you've been making against yourself, the more effective they'll be.

We also used symbolic imagery to combat Liz's negative self-statements. When we asked if she knew anyone who had absolute confidence in her ability to learn something new, she recalled Mindy, a dog she owned as a child. Mindy was always eager for new tricks, skills, and games, and was never daunted by failure. She'd just try again, always with her tail wagging. Imaging Mindy with her wagging tail, raring to give it another try, became Liz's shorthand for the traits she wanted to emulate.

Another way of dealing with negative self-statements is to increase your ability to accept positive messages from others. In our experience, most people who are negative about themselves have trouble hearing positive things from others. It's as if they're thinking, "I know I don't do anything right, so why should I believe you when you say I did?" Or "I know I'm no good, so why should I believe you when you say I am?" The partial or complete inability to accept compliments simply reflects a difficulty in believing good things about yourself, which itself is a consequence of repeatedly making negative self-statements.

As you start feeling better about yourself, it's easier to accept compliments. It also works the other way: the more you can accept positive comments others make about you, the more you can say similar things to yourself.

And by now you should know how to work on being able to receive compliments. Just relax and recall a compliment that was actually given to you and — this is the crucial part — imagine yourself accepting it gracefully, feeling calm and absolutely confident that what is said about you is true. You may have trouble with this at first, perhaps not quite being able to accept that this or that compliment is actually true. So accept it in part. Maybe you can't agree that your report or talk or whatever was wonderful or excellent, but maybe you can accept that it was acceptable or good or even very good. Practice this image as often as possible, until it's easy and totally acceptable. Then recall the real compliment and see if you can accept it as it was given. Maybe now wonderful or excellent will feel more comfortable. In the days and weeks you're imagining accepting compliments more gracefully, start talking to yourself more positively. Congratulate yourself for working on accepting compliments and give yourself a pat on the back whenever you do something well or better than before.

If you find that your accomplishments don't seem like quite enough because you're always comparing yourself to someone who does the same thing better, remind yourself that you're being silly. Making such comparisons is one sure road to eternal dissatisfaction. When the final accounting comes, no one is going to blame you for not writing as well as E. B. White, not being as bright and witty as Bertrand Russell, not looking like Jane Fonda, or not being as important a force for social change as Gloria Steinem. They may, however, ask why you weren't as good a you as you could have been.

Anytime you do something more quickly, more easily, more effectively, or more efficiently than before, that's cause for at least congratulations, maybe even for a celebration. The same holds anytime you make others feel better, do a service for your friends or community, or do something nice for yourself.

Our message about self-statements is really quite simple. There is nothing natural about sending nasty messages to yourself. If it feels natural, that's only because you've had so much practice doing it. The more you put yourself down, the worse you'll feel and the worse you'll do. Conversely, the more you say positive things to yourself, the better you'll feel and the better you'll do. It makes a great deal of difference what you say when you talk to yourself. You need to incorporate realistically positive self-statements in all your mental training and also in your dialogue with yourself at other times. In the long run, the goal is to substitute positive statements for negative ones. This goal takes months to achieve, but we've never had anyone say it wasn't worth the effort. Besides, some of the benefits are usually noticeable in a few weeks.

In summary, consider saying positive things to yourself. You might as well be nice and might as well program yourself for success rather than failure. It only requires a little extra effort.

*Man's mind stretched to a new idea never goes back to
its original dimensions.*

— Oliver Wendell Holmes

CHAPTER 11

USING POSTHYPNOTIC
SUGGESTION

A *posthypnotic suggestion* is a suggestion made in the relaxed state about something that you want to occur at another time. The words *when* and *as* are usually parts of
these suggestions. You have come across many examples
of the use of posthypnotic suggestion in earlier chapters —
every time we told someone that just as they succeeded in
X, they would now succeed in Y, and every time we suggested that such and such would happen at a time in the
future. Recalling past successes usually involves a posthypnotic suggestion: just as you once felt X, so you will
feel X when you next do Y.

Posthypnotic suggestion seeks to establish a new conditioned response to a situation or person or event that
was problematic and at least to neutralize counter-
productive responses (negative self-hypnosis). In the past,
for instance, you may have told yourself that as soon as
you got on the airplane, you would feel queasy and then
terror. Now we want to establish a new expectation:

As you take your seat on the plane, you will find yourself feeling as you do right now, very, very relaxed, very much at peace with yourself. You will enjoy looking around at your fellow passengers to see if there's anyone you know or might want to know. You may surprise yourself and start an animated conversation with one of your neighbors. Or maybe you'll get deeply involved in a book or magazine you brought along.

Most of process imagery can be thought of as posthypnotic suggestion, for as you imagine yourself being or acting in certain ways, you are indirectly suggesting to yourself that you will act and be in these ways under the appropriate circumstances. Posthypnotic suggestion is a more direct suggestive technique, often using more words than images, although it is always important to use as much imagery as possible.

We invariably ask someone to imagine the suggestion after it is given. Going back to our airplane example, after we gave the suggestion to feel more comfort, we would follow with something like this:

Now I'd like you to imagine yourself feeling just as you do now, very comfortable, very much at peace, walking down the aisle in the plane and taking your seat, feeling very relaxed. . . . . Splendid. And now imagine feeling curious, looking around to see if there's anyone you know on board or anyone you might want to know. Curious and very calm. . . . .

In process imagery, you imagine, step by step, the behavior you desire. In posthypnotic suggestion, you tell yourself that certain aspects of that behavior will occur at specified times. Process imagery and posthypnotic suggestion are merely different aspects of the same thing and work very well together.

One difference between these two techniques is that in process imagery you can, at least theoretically, imagine the entire process — every step and every word of giving a talk or running a race (though not, as we said, a marathon); every movement involved in throwing, catching, or hitting a ball; every aspect of selling more gizmos or writing more reports. Posthypnotic suggestion is more limited in that you can't have a suggestion for every part or aspect.

Posthypnotic suggestion therefore requires selectivity because you can only use one, two, or three for any given activity. You need to find the key element and make a suggestion from it. In the airplane example above, we and the client agreed that what she needed more than anything was a way of feeling comfortable at the start, as soon as she got in her seat. Recall our rule many chapters ago about using negative statements. They don't work well in mental practice; when you tell someone not to notice X or Y, they immediately notice it. So we worded our suggestions positively: instead of saying she wouldn't feel queasy or scared, we said she would feel relaxed, at peace, and curious. *Tell yourself what you will do or feel, rather than what not to do or feel.* (The indirect and unstated suggestion, of course, was that she wouldn't feel queasy and frightened.)

Cues for posthypnotic suggestion can be almost anything that occurs predictably before you want to carry out the suggestion. Athletes always lace up their shoes before practice and competition, so shoe-lacing can easily be used. Most of them put on uniforms as well, so that too can be used. "As you put on your shoulder pads [or shorts, T-shirt, or whatever], you can feel exactly as you do now, strong and sure, and fully confident in your abilities." Other examples are: "As you take the first steps up Heartbreak Hill, you can . . ."; "As you step onto the stage, you will

feel . . ."; "Whenever you meet a new man, you can . . .";
and "As you awaken in the morning, you can feel great
comfort and peace, looking forward to the day."

Notice that we have used the permissive "you can" in
most of our examples above and throughout the book.
Some people prefer the stronger "you will"; here as elsewhere, use what feels right to you.

In stage hypnosis, posthypnotic suggestions are usually
one-shot deals. The volunteer is told once or a few times
something like, "After you're back sitting in your seat and
I rub my ear, you'll experience a compelling need to sing
the national anthem and you will sing it." Posthypnotic
suggestion, as we use it, is very different. It is not a one-
time affair. It's something you'll want to repeat to yourself
while you're relaxed, many, many times over many days,
weeks, and perhaps even months. It will also grow out of
and be closely tied to your work with goal and process
imagery. You will, for example, imagine yourself doing
just what the suggestion tells you to do.

Posthypnotic suggestion works for the same reason that
other types of imagery and suggestion work. It reprograms
your mind and combats negative suggestion and imagery.
By suggesting over and over that you can feel or act in a
certain way in a certain situation, you are rehearsing doing
just that. You also make yourself feel better, knowing that
you will tend to be the way you want. Positive suggestion
and increased good feeling about yourself lead to confidence, and all of these things will help you do what you
desire.

Some words of caution, however. As with everything
else in this book, posthypnotic suggestion requires a heavy
dose of reality testing. If you've never given a public talk
before and you're terrified, and especially if you don't have
a lot of time to prepare with the various imagery techniques, it's probably asking too much that you be totally

relaxed and totally confident. But you can get around that by leaving out words like "totally" and "absolutely," and perhaps suggesting something like, "As you begin to talk, you may be surprised to find how quickly you relax, feeling calmer and calmer with each sentence you speak, and at some point realizing that you're doing just fine and maybe even enjoying it."

The rest of this chapter is a bit different from the preceding ones. We present two examples of the use of posthypnotic suggestions, as well as other techniques covered earlier, followed by an exercise to give you the structure for using such suggestions. But there is no script in that exercise. By now, you should be able to construct one on your own, using the examples in this and other chapters.

One of our clients, Tom, a top executive in a large company, wanted to learn to use a computer. Saying he wanted to learn is not quite accurate. He feared and disliked computers, mainly because he thought he had no mechanical aptitude and could never learn to use one correctly. Although he had a number of subordinates who could use the computer and get the information he required, he strongly believed it would be in his interests if he used it himself, particularly on weekends, when he often came in to play with new ideas. He didn't like having to wait a day or two until his "computer mavens" came in so he could ask them to get the information he needed.

The programs he wanted to learn, Lotus 1-2-3 and dBaseII, are too difficult for most people to learn on their own or from a book and for a number of reasons that need not concern us here, he eliminated a number of alternatives such as taking a class or getting private tutoring away from the office. There was no getting around it: Tom was going to have to take a course at work despite his fear of making mistakes and looking stupid in front of subordinates. His primary goal was to learn to use the computer in this course without humiliating himself in front of the other students.

Tom had, of course, taken many courses and seminars — often enjoying them and learning something useful. But since he had become a member of top management — "a heavy hitter," in his words — he felt that he didn't want to show his ignorance on any topic in front of subordinates. But his experience in previous courses was to be useful.

We had a long talk with Tom in which we sympathized with his fear of looking ignorant or stupid in front of subordinates and then told how we overcame the same problem. Being experienced therapists, we sometimes found ourselves in workshops with former students and even former clients. It wasn't easy at first, we informed him, but after getting over our initial fears and hesitation, we realized that everyone is ignorant about some things, that it's a sign of strength to be able to overcome the fear of looking stupid and taking the courses one needs, and that basically a course is just a course.

As with many of our clients, we wanted to enlist Tom's pride in his work. Pride is often taken as something sinful, something negative. To be sure, overweening pride is usually negative, but there is nothing wrong, and much good, about being proud of yourself and your work. We often find we can use this natural human tendency to good effect in our work — it can be a powerful motivator — and we commend it for your consideration.

We knew that although Tom feared looking foolish in front of subordinates, he was also critical of people at any level, including top executives, who stopped learning. He often made derogatory comments about Mr. X, who hadn't learned anything new in twenty years. He believed that a commitment to learning and improving yourself was important and he took pride in his efforts in this direction. We were to make use of this.

After Tom learned to relax, we made a tape for him that started by recalling a past success.

> As you sit there in the chair relaxing, you can recall X [a situation in the past where he felt very proud of what he had done]. That's right, allow the feelings of pride, of really feeling good about yourself, to permeate your whole being. . . . . Recall the details. Recall how good it feels to feel that good about yourself. . . . . Excellent. And let those feelings stay with you; just let them be there with you as we move along. Imagine yourself signing up for the Lotus course, feeling very proud of yourself, as proud as you now feel, for doing this. Remind yourself what a challenge it is for a heavy hitter to take a course with subordinates. It takes courage. It takes guts. It takes a man's man to take on a challenge like this. And you're showing the courage and the guts. . . . . Imagine the pride you'll feel. That's right. And now imagine the pride you'll feel as you leave your office to go to the classroom, as you take the elevator to the fourth floor — confident, relaxed, feeling very good about yourself, as good as you did when you did X — and now as you enter the classroom . . . . walk to a seat . . . . and sit down. Great.
>
> The more you imagine how good you'll feel when you sign up for the course and when you go to it and sit down in the room waiting for instruction to begin, the more vivid the experiences will be and the better you'll feel. You should listen to this tape every day, at least four times each day. And one more thing that will be of great interest to you. As you sign up for the course, every time you think about it, when you walk

into the room to take it, and as you sit down in your seat, you will feel exactly as you felt after X, you'll feel the same strength, the same pride, the same confidence that you are doing what is right and correct for you to do. As you sign your name on the list to indicate you'll take the course, you'll feel tremendous pride and satisfaction. As you leave your office to go to the course, you'll feel a tremendous sense of goodness about yourself. As you take the elevator and walk down the hall to the room, you'll feel more and more pride, confidence, and satisfaction. As you enter the room and take your seat, you'll know you're doing the right thing, feeling great pride, great strength, and very much at peace with yourself.

As Tom listened to the tape, his attitude changed somewhat in the right direction, but there was still his fear of computers. We knew he wouldn't actually sign up for the course until we did something about this. One day when he came into our office, he was surprised to see a computer sitting on the desk. We said we had been testing a new program, which was true, and wondered how easy it would be for a novice to learn one of its key operations, cutting and pasting a block of text. Tom was flabbergasted but agreed to help. We showed him how it was done and then guided him through the steps. It's a fairly simple operation when someone is showing you how. We went through it a number of times until Tom could do it with no help.

We asked how he felt now that he had mastered one of the most commonly used functions in the program. He was very surprised and didn't say anything for a few seconds. Then he blurted out, "I've got the smarts, I can do it." We quickly had him execute the cut-and-paste function a few more times and then taught him another one. We asked how he felt, and he said, "Better than I have in a long time. I'm getting to believe I can learn this stuff and there's even a sense of power about it, being able to make this machine do what I want." The careful reader can probably guess the next step.

We asked Tom to imagine having exactly the same feelings in the computer class as he had in our office and followed that up with a posthypnotic cue: "And as you sit in front of the computer in the class, listening to the instructor, you will feel exactly as you do here, confident, relaxed, powerful, and with increasing desire to learn more, knowing full well that you've got what it takes, you've got the smarts, you'll do it and do it well."

Some readers may be thinking that Tom was lucky because we got him to learn something on a computer almost before he knew what was happening, and that learning helped him achieve his goals. There is no question the learning helped, but anyone can ask a friend or colleague knowledgeable about computers to do exactly what we did: teach you one or two operations on a specific program. That usually gives the confidence to go on.

It would make a good story to say that Tom went on to become a computer buff and a teacher of courses on data base and spreadsheet programs, but that isn't what happened. For Tom, as for most people, computers and their programs were merely means to an end. He learned the programs he needed and used them in his work to get the data he required. This allowed him to be more efficient in his job — all that he really wanted. But he also came away from his experience with computer programs feeling much better about himself and his abilities.

Our next example concerns physical discomfort and pain. Although medicine has made great strides in the last thirty years, millions of people suffer from chronic pain and discomfort — from heart disease, back problems of many kinds, headaches, and so forth. Medicines help some of these people, but far from all. Many people cannot take painkilling medicines, while others can take them but find the side effects almost as bad as the original problem. The methods of mental training can often be a great help.

Before going on, we emphasize that anyone with physical pain should first consult a physician. We offer mental training as a supplement to good medical care, not as a substitute.

Almost all mental training can help in the relief of pain and discomfort. Relaxation itself is often very effective. Tension almost invariably increases the perception of pain. The more relaxed you are, the less discomfort you'll experience. Relaxation itself is often all that's needed to take care of what many now call tension headache, and it can also significantly reduce various back and other pains.

Goal imagery can be used to light the path: Imagine yourself already feeling more comfort, more energetic, healthier. Imagine your life as you now take walks with great comfort and ease, as you now cut the grass or work on the house with a sense of health and well-being. Whatever it is you'd like to be doing and however it is you'd like to be feeling as you do it, imagine yourself as already having achieved it.

Process imagery is very important for pain control. One thing you can do is imagine yourself engaging in desired activities while feeling great comfort and peace, enjoying yourself immensely. For some people, this might mean only walking around the house and to the grocery store. For others, it might mean sitting at a desk working. For still others, it might mean dancing or skiing. Whatever it is, you should fill your imagery with positive feelings of comfort, ease, energy, and well-being rather than give yourself suggestions about feeling less pain or use words saying that it won't hurt so much or it won't be so terrible this time.

Past successes and posthypnotic suggestions should be used. Recall how you felt before the injury or illness. Just as you felt so comfortable, so well when you took a walk then, so you can feel that way when you take a walk today. If that goal is too ambitious, then substitute something more appropriate; for example, "you can feel more like you did then when you take your walk today."

Process imagery can also be used to promote healing. Recall the example in the first chapter of Lonnie Barbach imaging her knee healing and becoming well — the ligaments getting tighter and the inflammation and redness decreasing. We are *not* implying that mental training can cure cancer or heart disease. But there is a great deal of evidence demonstrating that the mind's thoughts and images exert considerable influence on bodily disease. As we illustrated with another example in the first chapter, simple process imagery can increase the blood flow to suggested parts of the body. Increased blood flow means quicker healing, which in turn means less pain and discomfort. So imagine the increased flow of oxygen-rich, nutrient-filled, life-giving blood to the organ, tissue, or area that's problematic.

A similar process uses air. Several people with lower-back problems, for instance, have benefited from imagining breathing into their lower backs (a technique well known to people who make their living giving massages). This idea may sound a little strange, so here are the suggestions:

As you take a nice, deep inhalation, imagine the clean, healthy, healing air traveling right down into your back, bringing freshness and health with it. Imagine the air calming, cleansing, and healing the tissues. . . . . As you exhale, imagine the exhalation carrying out all unwanted feelings, and see them dissipating in the outside air . . . . , leaving you feeling cleaner, healthier, stronger, more relaxed, and the healing continues.

Much of the pain people feel is caused by the very medical procedures designed to help them. Surgery, needles, catheters, and the other accoutrements of medicine promote a lot of discomfort. Mental training can aid in dealing with them, as we illustrate with one of our own experiences in the next chapter.

We used posthypnotic suggestion with Paul, a musician who had pain in his lower back and one leg as a result of a herniated disk. Paul was under the care of several physicians but was unable to take the pain medicine they offered as it made him drowsy and unable to work effectively. All the methods of mental training were used to good effect. What follows are some of the posthypnotic suggestions. Please note that these were distributed over a number of sessions and tapes. We try not to do too much at any one time, a practice you should follow.

The first has to do with recalling a past success, a time when he had no back pain.

Recall once again how you felt two years ago when you played at Hertz Hall. Do you remember which piece was first, which second, which third? [This is just a prompt to get him to recall some detail about the experience.] . . . . Recall the feelings of ease, of strength, of competence, of joy in hearing the great sounds you're making. . . . . You really were having a ball. . . . . Remember how your legs felt, how your back felt as you sat down to play. . . . . Recall how the rest of your body felt as you began to play and continued playing. . . . . Felt so good you were hardly aware of your body, just aware of the music, the great sounds . . . . , and nice feelings of ease, strength, and joy. Hang on to those feelings because you can have them again. Just as you felt them when you played in Hertz Hall, just as you feel them now, you can feel them when you play tomorrow in your place. The same ease, the same strength, the same competence, the same joy. Just as you had these feelings when playing in Hertz Hall, you can have them again tomorrow. *Aware of your hands, aware of the music, aware of feeling terrific. Aware of the great music, great sound, and that's all you need to be aware of.* Exactly as it was in Hertz Hall.

The italicized sentences are indirect suggestions for Paul not to be aware of his back or leg. These kinds of suggestions work better than saying, "You won't be aware of your leg or back."

We used another kind of posthypnotic suggestion with Paul that is similar in some ways to the one above. He had lots of pain when walking, so we'd often have him imagine feeling comfort and ease when walking around the office. When he could vividly imagine doing that, we asked him to hold on to the feelings, get up, and walk around the office feeling exactly as he did in the imagery, always saying that he would be able to do so. This was then extended to walks down the hallway and then around the building.

We followed this up with walks in his environment — for instance, going to the post office. We had him imagine doing it feeling great comfort and very much at peace. When he indicated he could vividly imagine doing that, we would add something like this:

As it is in your mind, so it will be in the world. You can have the same easy feelings, the same comfort and peace that you're now experiencing, when you walk to the post office. You can feel just as relaxed, just as pleasant, just as comfortable walking to the post office as you're feeling right now. The feelings you're having right now will be the ones you'll have as you walk to the post office. Now let's imagine walking to the post office having exactly these same feelings of comfort and ease. . . . .

To be able to use posthypnotic cues effectively, you need to spend a few minutes, or perhaps a number of short sessions over several days, coming up with the basic ideas. Examples are wanting to feel more relaxed as you go to meet the customer, more focused as you sit down to study or write or begin to exercise, stronger and more confident as you talk to your boss, calmer and in control as you talk to your spouse, more organized as you take the examination, and so on. Once you have one or two items, write them down and leave them for a day or two. Then reread them and make any changes you desire.

The next thing is to word them properly. Always start with what you'll be doing or what will be happening, followed by what you want yourself to feel, think, say, or do; and use the by-now-familiar "As I [or when I] X, I'll feel [or be, say, or whatever] Y." Two examples are: "As I enter John's office, I'll feel at ease and at peace, eagerly anticipating the chance to bring the proposal to his attention"; "When I talk to Marti about my feelings of being misunderstood, I'll be very relaxed and feel very much in control, very strong, very good all over, just focusing on getting my complaints out as I had planned." And remember what we said at the beginning of the chapter. Always word your suggestions positively: tell yourself what you will feel or think or do, rather than what you won't feel or won't do.

Make sure that the cues and the suggestions are as accurate and specific as possible. If you have to walk up some stairs to get to the playing field or the boss's office, then imagine yourself walking up the stairs, feeling as you want to feel. If you take an elevator, then imagine doing that. Don't just magically appear on the field or in the office.

If you have a key word, phrase, or image, use it wherever you can fit it in.

Exercise 3: Using Posthypnotic Suggestions

Time required: 4 to 10 minutes

Make a tape that starts with some brief relaxation instructions and then goes on briefly to goal imagery or recalling a past success, followed by a posthypnotic suggestion you've settled on previously. Repeat the cue or suggestion several times duing the tape, using slightly different wording each time. Then use process imagery to imagine yourself doing precisely what it was you suggested you would do. If you suggested you would feel very calm as you took the exam, yet fully in touch with all your resources and knowledge, then imagine yourself feeling that way as you take the test. Imagining feeling something can be difficult, so it's always good to include some action that would reflect the feeling you want. For instance, you may think that someone who is calm and in touch with all his or her knowledge during a test would read every question carefully and then think about the answers. This is the action we're looking for. Imagine yourself reading each question carefully and then thinking about the answers before selecting one. Always end the process imagery with several more repetitions of the posthypnotic suggestion.

In general, the more you repeat the posthypnotic suggestions, the better, especially if you change the wording slightly on different repetitions. Aside from repeating suggestions, what you are saying over and over is a powerful kind of positive self-talk. You will know you are engaging in useless repetition when your mind wanders.

Tapes with posthypnotic suggestions, even including the appropriate process imagery, are usually brief (less than ten minutes, and often less than five after you've had some experience), which means you should listen to them at least four or five times a day.

* *

At times, you'll want to add other posthypnotic cues. Feel free to do so using the same guidelines and the information you've picked up about yourself the first time around. Make sure, however, not to use more than a few posthypnotic cues at any one time. Using too many will dilute their effect.

After you've listened to your tape with one posthypnotic suggestion for a few days (several times each day), start giving yourself the suggestion without using the tape. You'll probably be able to decrease the amount of time it takes to get relaxed and give the entire suggestion. When this happens, increase the frequency with which you do the exercise.

Summary: Guidelines for Using Posthypnotic Suggestion

• Make a short list consisting of one or two suggestions you'd like to give yourself regarding how to be, feel, think, or act in a certain situation. Be as accurate and specific as possible about the situation and how you want to be.

• Reword the suggestions using the "As I [or when I] X, I'll feel Y" construction. Word your suggestions positively (tell yourself what you can or will feel or do) and use key words and phrases.

• Make a tape that starts with brief relaxation instructions followed by either recalling a past success or goal imagery, and that then includes several repetitions of the posthypnotic suggestion. Then use process imagery to go over the situation feeling and doing what you suggested you would feel and do. End the tape with a few more repetitions of the posthypnotic cue.

• Listen to the tape as often as possible, at least four or five times a day. When you no longer need the tape (often after a few days of using it), continue using the suggestions without the recording, if possible decreasing the amount of time it takes and increasing the number of repetitions during a day.

• Don't totally neglect your goal imagery while working on posthypnotic suggestion. If you don't include goal imagery on your posthypnotic-suggestion tapes, use some brief goal imagery at least once or twice a week with or without a tape.

PUTTING IT ALL TOGETHER

In the next few pages, we present an example somewhat different from previous ones. It involves the feeling of anger, something many people have trouble with. We did not follow the therapeutic fashion of encouraging expression of the emotion. To the contrary, our goal, following the client's lead, was to block its expression, partly by giving her less reason to be angry. Anger is a common and complex emotion and we are not suggesting Cindy's ways of dealing with it are right for everyone. Her use of symbolic imagery, however, proved very valuable, both for increasing assertiveness and managing strong feelings; but each person has to come up with his or her own symbols.

Cindy's situation was complicated and she used lots of methods to deal with its many facets. We mention many of them to give you an idea of how to put together a program for yourself.

Cindy is a free-lance writer who was having considerable trouble with her husband, Greg, and her anger. She was doing all the housework, all the cooking, and all the caretaking of their two preadolescent boys. She often felt trapped, as if she existed only to take care of other people, and there never seemed to be enough time for herself. She was especially irritated about not having enough time for her writing, which was both a way of making money and of expressing herself.

Cindy usually just took care of everyone's needs without comment and then suddenly "got crazy," as she put it. She would go on screaming rampages and sometimes throw things at the boys or Greg. Several times she even hit them. In the last year, the anger started affecting her work. A few times she had lost control with coauthors and editors and lost writing assignments. She was concerned that she was developing a reputation as a problem writer and would have trouble getting assignments.

Her goals were to bring the anger under control and to have more time to write. She was stymied as to the means to these ends but vaguely realized that she had to tell Greg she wanted him to share equally in the housework and care of the children. We agreed that she needed to get more time for herself. If she didn't feel so powerless and used, she would have less anger to contend with.

Because we've already covered the development of assertiveness in our discussion of Charles in chapter 9, we needn't spend much time on it here except to note a few points. Cindy needed to have a discussion with Greg about what she wanted. We helped prepare her for it using almost all the methods previously discussed — goal and process imagery, positive self-talk, and posthypnotic suggestion. We did not, however, use a model, because Cindy came up with something more relevant to her situation.

She often mentioned not having the strength to talk firmly and persuasively to her husband. We asked if she had ever felt the kind of strength that would be necessary.

She replied that she had. In the two years after divorcing her first husband, she had felt very powerful. She had taken care of herself, had spent as much time as she wanted on her writing, and had gone out with lots of men, several of whom wanted to marry her. But she remained independent and in charge of her life. She spoke so movingly about herself at that time, we asked if an image came to mind. She answered in an instant: "I was a tigress. Strong, self-reliant, totally my own person." Many women we've worked with have reported a similar phenomenon: lots of strength and ability when on their own and a sudden loss of both when involved in a serious relationship with a man. And Cindy is one of several women to have spontaneously come up with the tigress image.

This image conveyed great strength to Cindy but she had largely forgotten it and the feeling. We had her bring it back many times every day. The effect was dramatic. As soon as she imaged the tigress roaming the jungle, she looked and sounded stronger. More important, she felt infused wih energy and power, especially when, at our suggestion, she merged into the image and saw the world through the tigress's eyes instead of looking at the animal from the outside. Cindy started almost all her mental training with the tigress image. After evoking this image, it was easy for her to imagine telling Greg what she wanted to tell him and to follow up until she reached her goals with him.

She soon had her talk — really a series of talks — with Greg, which went well. He was willing to do more work around the house, but suggested it would be easier on both of them to hire someone to come in twice a week to clean and do some cooking. In what was a surprise for Cindy, they came to the conclusion that the boys were being spoiled by all her attention and that they needed to be talked to about doing more work around the house and being less demanding. Greg wanted Cindy to talk to them, but she insisted they both do it, which they did a few days later.

Anyone who has tried to change the behavior of a spouse or child knows it does not go smoothly. Greg and the boys all tested Cindy's resolve in various ways. Although she wavered a number of times, recalling the tigress and how good she had felt when she was in control of her life carried her through. In a few months, her family got the message and things settled down to some extent.

Cindy was having fewer outbursts, but she was still having some and felt even worse because there was less provocation. In talking about this, we discovered that Cindy was following in her mother's footsteps. Her father was an ogre who permitted his wife little independence. But women did have the right to get crazy. So when Cindy's mother couldn't take it anymore, she really got crazy, throwing pots, dishes, and anything else she put her hands on.

Cindy did a lot of work on the anger. She told herself many times in trance that Greg was not like her father, that she need not act like her mother, and that she was free to act as she wanted. These things helped, but not enough. She still needed a specific instrument to block the growing anger. She ended up with two of them.

We asked Cindy to imagine her tigress acting the way she did. She couldn't: "A strong, independent animal wouldn't behave that way. She just takes care of business and doesn't have to act like that." So what business still needed taking care of? It turned out that Cindy felt deprived becase she didn't have a special place in which to write. She did her work on the dining-room table, where the boys and Greg often left mail and magazines, and even felt free to use her typewriter. When company came, she had to clear away her materials. "I want everyone to take me and my work seriously. I want an office of my own." We then elicited something she had wanted for years but had barely acknowledged even to herself: she wanted to convert the rarely used family room into her office.

It took only a few sessions with process imagery before she had a meeting with Greg and the boys and told them what she wanted. There were some objections, most of which Cindy had anticipated in her process imagery, but she prevailed when she said she would rent an office downtown if she couldn't have one in the house. This option had been worked on in her mental training. Cindy imaged the alternatives and realized that although she preferred to work at home if she could have the kind of setting she wanted, she would rather take an office elsewhere than continue at home under the old arrangement.

The other tool she used to deal with her angry feelings was more complex. We had her monitor her feelings over a period of weeks to determine what warnings she had that the anger was building. She came up with one very clear sign: an image of a huge freight train starting to roll down the tracks, quickly gathering momentum. When it was really moving, she got crazy. We had her imagine the train starting to roll and then asked her to imagine something stopping it, halting it in its tracks. She saw a huge hand, "like the hand of God," with the palm holding the train where it was and then pushing it back.

She imagined the whole scene many times each day: becoming aware of the train starting to move, seeing the hand come out of the sky to hold it in place and then push it backwards until it disappeared from view, leaving her feeling strong and calm like a tigress. Each time she imaged this scene, she gave herself the following suggestion: "As it now is in my mind, so it will be in the world. When I become aware of the train starting to move, I'll imagine the hand holding it and then pushing it back until the anger disappears. Good-bye anger, hello tigress. As it works in my mind, so it will work in the world."

And it did. Cindy had less reason to be angry. Greg and the boys were more respectful of her work, less demanding, and did more of their share. She had her own office and more time to write and do other things for herself. When she needed to be assertive with her family, the tigress was there to give her strength. We speculated that the main reason she still had angry outbursts was simply habit: she had seen her mother do it many times and had then practiced it herself over many years. The image of the giant hand stopping the train was sufficient to stop the outbursts before they went too far, leaving Cindy calm, strong, and able to get on with her work or determine if there was something that needed to be confronted.

We know that some people think that something as simple as the train image couldn't possibly be effective with as powerful an emotion as anger. We are in sympathy with that perspective because it used to be our own. Our attitude changed by observing the results of our work with Cindy and others. Simple images often have incredibly powerful consequences. We also want to repeat what we said before: It wasn't just the image that helped Cindy change. The other work she did to relieve her anger — for instance, getting her own office and demanding more time for herself — undoubtedly helped by giving her fewer reasons to be angry.

For readers who wonder where the anger went, or whether Cindy might be harming herself by not letting it out, we can only respond that such ideas are based on what is to us an antiquated notion of emotion — what might be called the teapot theory of anger. We refer interested readers to Carol Tavris's marvelous debunking of these ideas in her book *Anger*. Our experience is that people who learn to control or manage their anger suffer no negative consequences; on the contrary, they are invariably much happier, more satisfied, and more productive. This certainly was Cindy's experience.

Readers who want to emulate Cindy's work, whether to control angry outbursts or some other behavior, should keep in mind the principle we've illustrated a number of times: Use the stimulus that triggers the maladaptive response to trigger a different response. In the past, Cindy's freight train was simply allowed to gain momentum until she couldn't do anything about it. In her mental training, she kept the train but added something that would stop it. Charles in chapter 9 automatically said yes when anyone wanted something from him. He learned to anticipate the requests and replace yeses with nos for a large number of them. Same requests, but a different response to them. Dan, also in chapter 9, kept his mouth shut whenever he had an idea. He replaced nonexpression with expression. As soon as he had an idea, he gave voice to it. In all these cases, the same stimulus that triggered the unwanted behavior was conditioned through practice to trigger a more constructive behavior.

As Cindy had more time to work and experienced far fewer explosions of anger, the quality and quantity of her writing increased significantly, but one problem remained. A few months before she came to see us, Cindy had gotten into an angry altercation with an editor of a large and well-paying magazine. She very much wanted to write again for that magazine but was so embarrassed by her behavior that she couldn't imagine calling to apologize. Cindy's two images weren't any help. Tigers don't write and don't know anything about editors, and she couldn't think of a way to bring "the hand of God" into this. We should say, however, that what was true for Cindy isn't true for everyone. Imagery does not follow ordinary rules of logic and consistency. Mixed metaphors are commonplace, as are inconsistencies. Some people have imaginary animals who know a great deal about the world of writing, finance, or medicine. We even recall a man who got good advice on a manufacturing problem from some Conan-type figure from long ago. We don't understand it. All we know is that it worked.

One day Cindy said she wished she could consult a group of writers and editors for advice on what to do. So she assembled this group in her mind (a technique discussed in interlude 2), presented the problem, and asked for help. The unanimous suggestion of the group was the obvious one: write a letter of apology to the editor, taking full responsibility for the altercation, noting that she had worked hard and successfully on her anger, and requesting a chance to show what a good job she could do. Several members of her imaginary council of advisers suggested she end the letter with a proposal for an article she wanted to do, a suggestion she accepted.

The letter was not easy for Cindy to write because she felt so bad about her behavior with the editor. But the tigress gave her strength, as did recalling her recent successes with Greg and the boys. She went through several drafts before she was satisfied and then sent it. The outcome surprised us all. Cindy received a call from another editor, who said the first editor was no longer with the magazine. The editor calling said she had heard about the incident but, considering Cindy's letter, was willing to forget about it. And yes, she was interestd in Cindy's proposal but with some modifications. Cindy accepted and a contract was made.

Like all the examples we've presented, Cindy was a success. She largely got what she wanted, though not quite everything. Although Greg's behavior has changed considerably, especially regarding caring for the boys, he still isn't as involved in the housework as she would want and they occasionally do battle over this. But she's doing well with her writing, doesn't feel trapped, and rarely gets out of control. When she argues with Greg, she keeps her cool and is proud of how she conducts herself.

One thing we very much like about mental training is that although not everyone gets exactly what he or she wants, we've rarely encountered a situation where there weren't some valuable results. And that, we think, is saying something.

If one advances confidently in the direction of his dreams, and endeavors to live the life he has imagined, he will meet with a success unexpected in common hours.

— Henry David Thoreau

CHAPTER 12

THE REWARDS OF MENTAL TRAINING

Now that you've had some experience using your mind in more productive ways, we hope we can encourage you to continue doing so. As we said earlier, mental training is an invaluable tool for more effective living that you can use as often as you want. Some people use it more or less every day, while others use it only when something new, difficult, or threatening is in the offing.

There is hardly any situation in life that mental training can't help you deal with in a better, more constructive, and healthier way. No matter what you do, your mind is going to deal with every situation in one manner or another. Why not take steps to ensure that it works to your best advantage?

Years of training and experience with all kinds of therapeutic approaches have convinced both of us that the methods discussed in this book are the most useful. Many other consultants, therapists, and physicians have come to the same conclusion. We have to admit that sometimes we're even a bit embarrassed about these techniques. After all, mental training is so simple and easy when compared to most other therapeutic methods that it seems incomprehensible that it works so well. Something this effective should be harder, we sometimes think. But then we have occasion to use one or more of the techniques with clients or in our own lives and once again surprise ourselves: simple or not, this stuff really works. When preparing to see an especially difficult client, when delivering a lecture to a large audience, when feeling inexplicably tense or irritable, when embroiled in a professional debate, when dealing with an uncooperative colleague or an unhelpful sales clerk, when undertaking a new project — at all these times and on many other occasions, we employ imagery, rehearsal, posthypnotic suggestion, and so forth.

To illustrate how we ourselves use the methods we have presented in this book, we offer recent examples from each of our lives.

Last year, AAL had to undergo minor surgery — a transurethral resection of the prostate (TURP). Although this is not a major or life-threatening procedure, it nevertheless involves a five- to six-day stay in the hospital, replete with the usual postoperative intravenous drips, catheters, antibiotics, and other medical interventions. Aside from all this, AAL has a longtime distrust and dislike of doctors; thus any medical procedure for him is not undertaken lightly or easily.

AAL's goals were to make the experience as pleasant and healing as possible, with a minimum of anxiety. The first thing he did was to collect information on exactly what would transpire: the hospital admission process, the preoperative preparations, the surgical procedure, and what would go on postoperatively. Some doctors and nurses are inclined to sidestep these issues. "Don't worry, it will all be taken care of. When the time comes, you will be told exactly what to do." Some patients prefer it this way, but for those like AAL who feel better knowing in advance what each step entails, it is often necessary to be assertive and firm, even adamant. "I want to know *now* so that I can prepare myself and be absolutely sure that I am truly good and ready when the time comes."

Starting about ten days before the operation, AAL carefully visualized each step in the process several times a day, using appropriate posthypnotic suggestions to the effect that he would feel comfortable, calm, somewhat detached, and curious. The goal here was to achieve a positive mental state and reduce anticipatory anxiety. The first step was imagining the trip to the hospital. Next, the admission process was attended to and then the focus changed to images of being in the hospital bed, watching TV, reading, and dwelling on enjoyable activities. The visualizations produced clear images of proceeding through each step with interest and curiosity rather than fear and dread. Day by day, the relaxation and images reduced the usual tensions and anxieties.

The ten days of mental training had the desired effect. AAL felt calm detachment as he actually went to the hospital, checked in, went to his room, undressed, got into bed, and was shaved by the attendant.

While lying in the hospital bed the night before surgery, he made use of relaxation, positive imagery, posthypnotic suggestion, and positive self-talk ("It's going to be just fine"; "It will be over before you know it"; "In a few weeks, you'll barely be able to remember any of this"). Significantly, he found a book of mystery stories so absorbing that around midnight a nurse had to suggest that he go to sleep since the surgery was scheduled for 7:30 A.M. The self-help techniques combined with his powerful absorption in the mysteries had produced a temporary amnesia — he had totally forgotten about the impending operation.

While being wheeled into the operating room, AAL made

extensive use of slow abdominal breathing, relaxation, and positive self-talk. Since he had agreed with the doctors on a spinal anesthetic rather than a general one, he was wide awake the whole time. The predominant emotion was one of remarkable tranquility and he chatted throughout with the surgeon, the anesthesiologist, and the nurses. After the surgery, in the recovery room, he made additional use of slow, deep breathing and calming images.

AAL's main postsurgical concern was the pain that might develop when the anesthetic wore off. Consequently, he used healing imagery (pictures of the surgical site healing rapidly, being clean and healthy-looking) and distraction (fantasizing having adventures in all sorts of places other than a hospital). His main feeling was one of discomfort rather than pain, except for an excruciating headache that proved incapacitating whenever his head was raised more than twenty-five degrees. (A small percentage of patients develop a post-spinal-anesthetic headache that can last for many days.)

Since not even the imagery could combat that pain, he had to lie on the bed with his head flat for several days, which alleviated the pain but produced boredom because he could not read, watch TV, or walk. The cure, of course, was directly at hand. The beauty of mental imagery is that with one's eyes closed, it is possible to take exciting trips into the past, into the future, and into any imagined — or previously unimagined — spot in the universe. AAL is not willing to disclose all his adventures, but it was clear that he felt fine most of the time and didn't even seem to mind being in one of his least favorite places, a hospital.

Once he could raise his head without bringing on a headache, life got much easier even though he was housebound for several weeks. There was plenty of work to be done. Indeed, this book was high on his agenda at the time. He bought a computer, learned to use it, and one of the first projects to emerge from it were his contributions to this book.

For someone with such intense negative feelings about medicine, surgery, and hospitals, this experience was as positive as could be expected. The support of friends and a loving family were, of course, invaluable, but AAL gives a lot of credit to the mental training for bringing him through it so well. And he's far from the only one. We know scores of people who've made surgery and other medical procedures much more pleasant and much more comfortable by using the techniques of mental training.

BZ used many of the same methods to deal with one of the most difficult situations he has had to confront, the impending death of his father. The situation was complicated because of the consequences of the death of his mother when he was twelve. Although he had some knowledge that his mother was dying, his twelve-year-old mind couldn't cope with it and ended up denying reality. The denial continued when she died. He felt no sadness and cried no tears, not even at her funeral. In fact, he looked around in amazement at the people who were crying at the funeral. He couldn't figure out what was wrong with them. This denial was to have long-lasting negative effects.

As an adult, BZ formed a loving though often stormy relationship with his father. They became close and were able to talk as never before, to hug and kiss, and to exchange verbal expressions of love and appreciation. And then his father's heart started to deteriorate seriously. Since his father was seventy-five, had a history of heart trouble, and could not tolerate most medications, it was clear that his death would not be far off.

BZ had several goals in this situation. One of them was to be as supportive as possible of his father. One means to that end involved making a number of tapes for him (using the same techniques we've given in this book) to help him sleep, to ease his pain, and to let him know how much he meant to his eldest son.

Another means was to avoid upsetting his father. BZ's family was one where conflicts and arguments were never far away. BZ ideally wanted no fights at all, but realistically was willing to settle for a reduction in their frequency and intensity. To help achieve this goal, he used process imagery for at least a week before every visit home, going over all the stimuli that usually caused trouble and imagining himself responding differently to them. He also imagined recovering more quickly in case a conflict did occur. It would be satisfying to report that there were no upsets at all in the year-long period we are discussing, but that wasn't the case. Mental training isn't magic. But it helped nonetheless. Despite the very high level of tension that almost necessarily accompanies this kind of situation (which included numerous hospitalizations, quintuple bypass surgery, and trials with every known heart drug), and despite the fact that the whole family was haggard and often on the edge of hysteria, there were only a few conflicts and most were quickly resolved or at least covered over.

BZ's other goal was to ensure that he didn't repeat what he had gone through at his mother's death. No denial this time, no pretending that no one was dying, that no one had died. BZ was concerned that if he waited until the day of his father's death, he might freeze up as he had done many years before. He had to acknowledge his father's death before it happened.

Over a period of months, he imagined a number of scenes that indicated his father was dead. Since he had for many years called his father every Sunday, he imagined himself picking up the phone, starting to dial, and then realizing sadly that there was no one to call. At other times, he imagined feeling very lonely when his next book came out, unable to send the first copy to his father for his approval. He also imagined his father's body cold and stiff, with the life gone out of it. In what was to be the hardest scene for him, he imagined shaking his father's cold body, begging him to wake up, and getting no response except the sound of his own crying.

These sessions were not easy. BZ usually sobbed his way through them, feeling sad and alone. But they had the intended effect. Over several months' time, he gradually accepted the fact of his father's impending death. When the fateful call came one morning, he knew as soon as the phone rang what the message was. There was pain and there was sadness, but this time reality was faced. Now, over a year later, there is still pain and sadness at times. Some of the images BZ employed have been lived out. He often has lifted the phone on Sunday and started to dial, then sadly replaced it. And he did have a new book come out, feeling lonely when he received his copies, knowing that his father would have taken great pride and pleasure in it, as he did in the accomplishments of all his children.

Whatever the long-term outcome of this event for BZ, it is clear it will be a lot better than what happened after the death of his mother. His use of mental imagery helped him face a fact that absolutely had to be faced. The death of loved ones is never easy to face, but denying it is even worse. Although BZ still misses his father, he is grateful to the techniques that helped him handle his father's death in a healthy way and to those who helped him learn these methods.

We do not wish to end on a sad note. Sometimes facing life is more difficult than facing death. Even the great challenges and opportunities — the ones that can bring joy, pride, satisfaction, and other rewards if properly navigated — are extremely difficult to confront at the moment. A vast array of methods are available to deal with such situations and to cope with the vagaries of life. Many of them do not work and do not help; others can help but are so much trouble it's unclear if they're worth it.

We have found the techniques in this book to be both amazingly effective and easy to use. We like their utility and we like the fact that they simply employ your natural abilities and are not dependent upon external supervision. Once you have the basic ideas, you can adapt the techniques in whatever ways best suit your situation, your life, yourself. And once you get the basic ideas down, their proper application takes very little time. We also like the continuing learning about yourself that goes on as you use them. Whether in working with others or with ourselves, we're often surprised to find that a new key word or image is more effective than one we've been using, or that a different way of phrasing a suggestion works better for a certain problem or person. We've also found a great deal of humor and delight in these techniques. It can be uproariously funny to discover what ridiculous ideas our minds sometimes grasp, and delightful when a way is found to loosen that grip. And some of the images we use are in themselves a delight.

We hope you'll give the methods a try if you haven't already done so and that you'll continue to use them if you have. We are sure you'll find them as beneficial as we and thousands of others have.

Why not use the natural powers of your own mind to your best advantage?

SUGGESTED READING

Achterberg, J. *Imagery in Healing.* New Science Library, 1985.

Alberti, R. E., and Emmons, M. L. *Your Perfect Right: A Guide to Assertive Living.* Impact, 1986.

Bennis, W., and Nanus, B. *Leaders: The Strategies for Taking Charge.* Perennial, 1985.

Burns, D. *Feeling Good: The New Mood Therapy.* Signet, 1980.

Garfield, C. *Peak Performance: Mental Training Techniques of the World's Greatest Athletes.* Tarcher, 1984.

―――. *Peak Performers: The New Heroes of American Business.* Morrow, 1986.

Green, E., and Green, A. *Beyond Biofeedback.* Dial, 1977.

Kriegel, R., and Kriegel, M. H. *The C Zone: Peak Performance under Pressure.* Fawcett, 1984.

Lazarus, A. A. *In the Mind's Eye: The Power of Imagery for Personal Enhancement.* Guilford, 1984.

Naisbitt, J., and Aburdene, P. *Re-inventing the Corporation.* Warner, 1985.

Nicklaus, J. *Golf My Way.* Simon and Schuster, 1974.

Peterson, G., and Mehl, L. *Pregnancy as Healing*, vol. 1. Mindbody Press, 1984.

Russell, B., and Branch, T. *Second Wind*. Ballantine, 1979.

Samuels, M., and Samuels, N. *Seeing with the Mind's Eye*. Random House, 1975.

Schwarzenegger, A., and Hall, D. *Arnold: The Education of a Bodybuilder*. Pocket Books, 1982.

Sheikh, A. A., ed. *Imagery*. John Wiley, 1983.

———. *Imagination and Healing*. Baywood, 1984.

Soskis, D. A. *Teaching Self-Hypnosis*. Norton, 1986.

Tavris, C. *Anger: The Misunderstood Emotion*. Simon and Schuster, 1982.

Woolfolk, R. L., and Lehrer, P. M., eds. *Principles and Practice of Stress Management*. Guilford, 1984.

Zilbergeld, B., Edelstien, G., and Araoz, D., eds. *Hypnosis: Questions and Answers*. Norton, 1986.

Dear Reader:

As mentioned in the text, we have prepared two audio tapes using multitrack recording and other technology that can significantly increase your success with mental training. Descriptions of these products can be found on the facing page along with ordering information.

Our work continues and we would like to hear from you. We invite you to write to us about your experiences with mental training — our methods, those of others, and those you've developed on your own. We guarantee anonymity if we use anything you say.

We'd also like to keep you informed of what we're doing. If you'd like to be on our mailing list — to learn of future talks, books, video materials, and other audio cassettes as they are completed — please send us a card and say that's what you want.

To be on our mailing list or tell us of your experiences, write us at:

MindPower Distribution Services
2847 Shattuck Avenue
Berkeley, CA 94705

Mind Power on Tape

Tape 1: A 90-minute cassette of the exercises in *Mind Power* that makes full use of the audio medium, including music, multiple voices, and multitrack recording. The enhancements bring a greater efficacy to the exercises than is possible with simpler reproduction techniques. The tape is designed to be used in your own mental-training program. Price: $9.95 (plus $1.50 shipping and handling)

Tape 2: Actually a set of two 90-minute cassettes containing the essence of *Mind Power* but without the exercises. Listening to this dynamic presentation — which uses the same audio enhancements as Tape 1 — will add significantly to your understanding of mental training and your abilities with it. Price: $16.95 for the two-cassette package (plus $2.00 shipping and handling)

Tape 1 and Tape 2: We pay shipping and handling if you order both tapes. Price: $26.90

To order tapes: Send a check or money order for the full amount (California residents add 6% sales tax), made out to "MindPower," to the above address; or send your VISA or MasterCard information (card number, expiration date) and your signature. Credit-card customers can also order by calling (415) 839-4200.

Please send all inquiries about tapes to us, not to Little, Brown and Company.